FRESH
Chef on the Run

Diane Clement

Copyright Diane Clement, 1990.

Sunflower Publications
1426 West 26th Avenue,
Vancouver, British Columbia,
Canada. V6H 2B4

All rights reserved. No part of this book may be reproduced in any form by any means without permission in writing from the publisher, except by a reviewer who may quote brief passages in a review.

Canadian Cataloguing in Publication Data

   Clement, Diane, 1936–
     Fresh! : chef on the run
     ISBN 0-920120-05-9
     1. Entertaining. 2. Menus. 3. Cookery.
   I. Title.
   TX731.C443   1990   641.5   C90-091590-0

Editing by Liz Bryan
Photography by Jack Bryan
Typeset by The Typeworks
Printed and bound in Canada by Mitchell Press Ltd., Vancouver

Table of Contents

Prologue   1

THE MENUS
  Cucina Rustica   3
  Weather or Not   10
  Mid-East/Moroccan Melange   21
  Entertaining Santa Fe Style   29
  Breakfast of Champions   36
  The Big Production   43
  Portable Pleasures   49
  Halibut Mango Tango   58
  Shades of Summer   64
  Apres Ski   67
  Mexican Quesadillas Brunch   71
  Just in Case   75
  Something to Celebrate   81
  Pasta, Pasta, Pasta!   93
  Orient Expression   101
  Cross Culture Cuisine   106

Drop over for Brunch!   112
  A Trio of Souffles   120
  Break an Egg!   129

Global Food
  A Glossary of Exotic Items   153

The Well-Stocked Pantry   158

Index of Recipes   162

To the family:
Rand and Pati Matheson,
Maurice and Pat Clement,
the Chieftains of our high-spirited clan
for their endless love
and encouragement

Prologue

This book is the fourth in the Chef on the Run series. Like the others, it features complete menus designed primarily for entertaining, though on the whole I think the recipes themselves are simpler and certainly draw more heavily on ethnic influences. As with the other books, many of the recipes can be made ahead of time and many are real quickies that you can have on the table ready to eat in well under an hour, starting from scratch. And to help you get organized, each menu comes with a count-down plan to help you through the preparation stages. Often, it's the timing, not the cooking, that's tricky.

Because much of the entertaining of the 90s will tend, I think, to be of a more casual nature, I have included a whole big chapter on The Brunch, with lots of recipes where the guests themselves can lend a hand. If your kitchen is anything like mine, it's where the guests like to congregate, so if they're there, then put them to work. They'll love it!

Also, in answer to reader demand, I've included a suggested list for stocking up an emergency shelf so that you will never be at a loss for something tempting to serve when friends drop in for dinner without warning.

The recipes in this book, though most of them are part of a set menu, are designed to be mixed and matched according to your whim, with others in this book, and with those in my three other books. In other words, I hope you will create your own unique menus by taking an appetizer from here, an entree from there, a salad from the Family Favourites, and a dessert from somewhere else. And you can also just cook the main course, and fill out the extra with specialties from your favourite deli. I do this often.

Over the years it has become a lot easier, at least in Vancouver, to be a creative cook without spending all your time shopping or in the kitchen. Suddenly, it seems, there are delis and gourmet take-outs and specialty food shops on every corner, most of them first class. I take full advantage of them, stopping on my way home for a special salad or a dessert, a pasta sauce or some fresh salsa to round out the family meal. And if I'm really squeezed for time, I've been known to bring home enough items for a complete meal!

There are also many more sources for fresh produce and exotic food items than ever before. Granville Island Market and the other farmer's markets in Richmond, New Westminster and the North Shore are all wonderful places to shop for their atmosphere, colour and variety. They provide a most important ingredient: inspiration. Because I live in Kerrisdale I do much of my shopping at one of Vancouver's oldest produce markets, J.B. Hoy's on West 41st Avenue, a family concern that has been seeking out the freshest and best for more than 65 years. Girlie Koo, husband Allan and sons Ted and Bob continue to give personal service and somehow find time to chat with everyone. Their produce is perfection — there's always something new to taste — and their dedication is rare. I look forward to my visits.

The 90s, I think, will continue to see a concern with healthy eating; less fat, sugar, salt and eggs, more whole grains, fruits and vegetables. I also think we will see a big return to home entertaining around the dining table with friends and family. And the family Sunday dinner may make a comeback. These are the occasions to splurge, to make that favourite apple pie or that rich and meaty soup, that egg-rich souffle or sweet, liqueur-laden special cake. If we eat sensibly the rest of the week — and keep up the exercise — we can all afford to consume a few extra calories once in a while.

The photographs in this book show the food exactly as it was prepared (and afterwards eaten.) I don't believe in faking things for the sake of a good photo. Taking the photos was actually the fun part of the book. We invited friends over to watch Jack at work and to help us eat it all afterwards. We can honestly say that everything shown in the book has been thoroughly taste-tested.

I sincerely hope this new book will inspire you to take the time to enjoy two of life's many pleasures: cooking and eating, with your friends and family.

Diane Clement

Acknowledgments

I thank all the following for their enthusiasm and help in so many ways:

Barb Crompton and Julie McNeney, The Fitness Group; Vicki Gabereau, Fanny Kiefer, Rosemary Allenbach and Patrick Munroe, the CBC; Barb McQuade, the Vancouver Sun; Elizabeth Baird, Canadian Living; Glenys Morgan, The Market Kitchen (for striking dishes and table accessories); her cooking school coordinators Arden Narusevicius and Karen Neilson; Patty Howden, The Kitchen Shelf; Cindy Evett and Rhonda Ceci, Tools & Techniques; Eileen Dwillies, Eileen's Creative Cooking; Diana Becker and Ann Merling, Pierre Dubrulle's Culinary School; Don and Marcelle McLean and Haik Gharibian for recipes and food photography in their homes; cooking school students and friends for the food testing; my family Doug, Jennifer (who designed the smashing shirt on the front cover) and Rand; Suzanne Campbell and Jamie Norris — I thank you all.

Cucina Rustica Italy's Country Cooking

Assorted Crostinis
(Bruschetta, Pesto, Chevre, Mango & Prosciutto)
Warm Spinach Salad with Prosciutto
Risotto Al Frutti de Mare
(Seafood Risotto)
Focaccia Bread
Tiramisu
(Pick Me Up)

The Italians feel that cooking is like love: there are no rules and everything should be done with feeling. I fell in love with the simple, robust food of the Tuscany region in the heartland of Italy. Here, the cooks use local natural ingredients to produce specialties that are strongly flavoured, yet never spicy or heavy. They are a perfect marriage to the local wines: Chianti Classico is my choice.

Countdown

Several days ahead: Prepare spinach greens and refrigerate; toast pine nuts and refrigerate; grate Parmesan cheese; make Chevre-Ricotta spread.

A day ahead: Make Tiramisu; chop vegetables and cook first stage of Risotto dish; grill bread for Crostini.

On day of serving: In the morning, prepare Spinach Salad dressing; Bruschetta and Mango and Prosciutto Crostini; prepare rest of ingredients for Risotto.

Assorted Crostini

These little titbits are usually served as a complementary appetizer at most trattorias and they go well with the regional house wines. They are simply thin slices of day-old Italian or French bread which have been crisped under the grill to serve as bases for tasty toppings. Fettuntas are crostini which have been rubbed with a little oil and garlic before grilling. Both can be made the day of serving.

I usually use a French baguette loaf. Set oven to broil. Slice one or more loaves about ⅓ inch (8 mm) thick, place on a cookie sheet and broil on both sides for a few minutes until golden. You can also grill them on the barbecue. For Fettuntas, brush both sides of each slice of bread with olive oil and rub with a peeled garlic half before cooking. Keep cooked crisps in a basket until ready to spread with the toppings.

Bruschetta

This combination of raw tomatoes, fresh basil, olive oil and vinegar is known throughout Tuscany. For best results, it should be prepared the day of serving. Keep at room temperature and strain some of the excess juice from the mixture before serving. Bruschetta can also be served in place of the salad course.

Serves 8 to 10 on Crostini for appetizers, 6 as salad.

> 2½ cups (625 mL) *Roma or regular tomatoes, cut into small chunks*
> 8 to 10 *sun-dried, oiled tomatoes, chopped (optional)*
> ½ cup (125 mL) *finely chopped green onion*
> ½ cup (125 mL) *fresh basil leaves, cut into thin strips (or 1 teaspoon (5 mL) dried basil)*
> 2 or more *cloves garlic, crushed or minced*
> 1 tablespoon (15 mL) *Balsamic or red wine vinegar*
> 2 tablespoons (30 mL) *olive oil*
> Pinch *salt if desired*
> Pepper

Discard seeds from chopped fresh tomatoes and drain well. Mix everything together and let sit at room temperature for several hours. Serve on top of crostini, topped with a leaf of fresh basil.

Bruschetta is delicious by itself but this cheese mixture spread onto the crostini before you add the tomato mixture makes an interesting change of pace.

1 cup (125 mL) creamy ricotta cheese
½ cup (125 mL) mild creamy chevre (goat cheese)

Mix both cheeses together and refrigerate. This can be made well ahead. Add a little chopped green onions and basil.

To serve: I like to put a mound of the cheese spread in the centre of a flat tray, surround the cheese with a circle of bruschetta, provide plenty of crostinis and let guests help themselves. Garnish the tray with fresh basil leaves and serve with assorted Greek and Italian marinated olives.

Pesto Crostini

The combination of pesto and goat cheese baked on small wedges of rye bread is very tasty. Serve these crostinis with soup or salad or just by themselves as appetizer or snack. If you haven't time to make your own pesto (which is simply a mixture of fresh basil, olive oil, garlic and pine nuts, pounded together in a pestle), pick some up at a deli. It keeps well in the freezer.

Prepare the crostinis as before, but using light rye bread cut into small thin wedges, and grill on both sides. Spread each with a thin layer of pesto and top each with a small piece of goat cheese. Bake at 400 degrees F. (200 degrees C.) for about 5 minutes until warmed through. Serve immediately.

For a change, place some chopped sun-dried tomatoes on top of the cheese before baking.

Toasted Sesame/Chevre Crostini

Toast about ½ cup (125 mL) sesame seeds in an ungreased skillet, stirring constantly. Set aside. Cut chevre or goat cheese into small pieces to fit the crostini. If desired, have on hand some strips of sun-dried, oil-soaked tomatoes.

Just before serving, roll the cheese pieces in the toasted sesame seeds and place one on top of each crostini. Top with a strip of sun-dried tomato and place on cookie sheet. Bake at 400 degrees F. (200 degrees C. for about 5 minutes, or until warmed through. Serve immediately.

Note: Red or yellow peppers sliced into thin strips could be used instead of the sun-dried tomatoes.

Crostini di Mango and Prosciutto

This is simple, but just wonderful, a Tuscan specialty! Combine a little soft butter with a few chopped thin slices of prosciutto and a few slices of ripe mango. Puree in food processor and serve in very thin layer on crostini.

Warm Spinach Salad with Basil and Prosciutto

A hint of the Orient (rice wine vinegar) infiltrates the zesty Italian ingredients to add an intriguing sweet/sour taste.   Serves 6.

> 6 cups (1.5 L) prepared spinach
> ¾ cup (180 mL)olive oil
> 2 cloves garlic, chopped
> 3 tablespoons (45 mL) shallots, finely chopped
> 4 to 5 tablespoons (60 to 75 mL) diced prosciutto, fat removed
> 4 to 5 tablespoons (60 to 75 mL) rice wine vinegar (or red wine vinegar)
> 2 to 3 tablespoons (30 to 45 mL) chopped fresh basil
>   (or ¼ teaspoon (1 mL) dried basil)
> 4 tablespoons (60 mL) toasted pine nuts
> 2 to 3 tablespoons (30 to 45 mL) freshly grated Parmesan cheese
> Fresh pepper

The greens can be prepared and the pine nuts toasted a day or two ahead. Both will keep fresh in the refrigerator.

To make the dressing: Heat olive oil in small skillet, add garlic, shallots and prosciutto and saute until shallots are limp. Add vinegar, basil and pepper. Keep warm. (The dressing can also be made a day ahead, refrigerated, then reheated.)

To serve: Toss the spinach greens with enough warm dressing to coat leaves evenly. Divide among six salad plates and sprinkle the pine nuts and grated cheese on top.

Note: Prosciutto is a salted and air-dried ham available in most delis but you can use Canadian back bacon instead.

Risotto al Frutti de Mare
(Seafood Risotto)

A fine main dish to prepare in front of friends. Have everything ready before your guests arrive, give them a glass of wine and let them help with the stirring. The dish requires a stubby grain rice known as Arborio, which can be found in Italian specialty stores. Risotto is not the same without it. Take the time to try this dish—it is sure to become one of your classic recipes and the ingredients can be altered to suit the season and your tastes. Serves 6 as main course.

2 to 3 tablespoons (30 to 45 mL) butter
½ cup (125 mL) finely chopped onions
4 tablespoons (60 mL) finely chopped shallots (or use green onions)
2 cloves garlic, crushed
1 carrot, peeled and finely chopped
2 sticks celery, finely chopped
About 1 teaspoon (5 mL) finely chopped fresh ginger root
1½ teaspoons (7 mL) Tandoori powder (Sherwoods) (or 1 teaspoon (5 mL) mild curry powder
1½ cups (375 mL) wild or regular mushrooms, sliced
2 cups (500 mL) raw Arborio rice
7 to 8 cups (1.75 to 2 L) chicken stock
1 cup (250 mL) dry white wine
About 1½ cups (375 mL) freshy grated Parmesan cheese
½ lb (250 g) each of peeled prawns, halved scallops and cubed salmon

On the morning of serving, or the night before, heat the butter in a heavy skillet and add onions, shallots, garlic, carrots, celery and ginger root. Saute for a few minutes until golden and translucent. Add the Tandoori powder and mushrooms and saute for an additional few minutes. Add rice and stir until rice is opaque. Put dish aside until 30 minutes before serving.

Heat chicken stock and keep warm To the skillet, add the dry white wine and about 1 cup (250 mL) of the warm stock. Stir constantly until stock is absorbed, but don't let the rice stick. Keep adding stock, about ½ cup (125 mL) at a time, stirring all the while, until there is about 1½ cups (375 mL) of stock left in the bottom of the pan (about 5 minutes before dish is complete).

Add seafood and stir gently until seafood is opaque and almost all the liquid absorbed. Rice should be tender, though slightly firm to the bite, and mixture creamy. Add about 4 tablespoons (60 mL) cheese, pepper to taste. Serve immediately with more cheese for topping. The dish should take 25 to 30 minutes to complete. Don't rush it.

Note: Fresh asparagus or snow peas are pleasant accompaniments. Any leftovers can be reheated like a pancake in a non-stick frypan. Flip over once, sprinkle with Parmesan cheese and serve in wedges. Great for breakfast!

Tiramisu
(Pick Me Up)

This is Monique Barbeau's great version of the Italian classic dessert which originated in the royal courts of Siena in the 18th century. Containing lots of espresso coffee, Marsala and chocolate, it is guaranteed to "pick you up". Similar to the classic English trifle, it uses Mascarpone cheese as well as zabaglione custard. This cheese is similar to cream cheese but sweeter. Look for it in specialty cheese shops. A combination of lightly whipped cream and sweet ricotta or cream cheese would make a good substitute. Marsala is an Italian dessert wine similar to a sweet sherry. It can also be served over ice as an aperitif.

Serves 12.

Zabaglione

3 large egg yolks
3 tablespoons (45 mL) white sugar
⅓ cup (80 mL) Marsala
1 egg white, beaten thick

¼ cup (60 mL) strong espresso or regular coffee
8 ounces (250 g) mascarpone cheese, at room temperature
1 pint (500 mL) whipping cream, whipped
Approx. 4 dozen small ladyfingers (from Italian specialty shop)
Approx. 1 cup (250 mL) Marsala
4 oz (120 g) semi-sweet chocolate, grated

First make the custard: In a large shallow stainless steel mixing bowl beat the egg yolks and sugar until lemon coloured. Add ⅓ cup (80 mL) Marsala and whisk thoroughly. Place the bowl in a large saucepan of simmering water—the water should just touch the bowl—and beat rapidly with a wire whisk for a few minutes. The custard should soon thicken. Set bowl aside to cool. Fold in the stiffly beaten egg white.

In a separate bowl, whip the coffee into the mascarpone cheese and gradually fold in the whipped cream. Set aside.

To assemble: Dip the ladyfingers very quickly into the remaining 1 cup (250 mL) of Marsala. Don't let them soak up too much. Put a single layer of the moistened ladyfingers on the bottom of a lasagne-sized pan and spread over about half of the zabaglione. Cover with half the mascarpone cheese/cream mixture; repeat layers, ending with the cheese mixture. Sprinkle with an even layer of grated chocolate and refrigerate for several hours or overnight. Cut into small squares to serve. This goes very well with fresh berries.

Weather or Not

Champagne
Triple Creme Cheese with Mangoes and Strawberries
or Baked Brie
Wild Rice Salad
Steamed Nova Scotia Lobster with Fresh Chive
or Lemon Dill Mayonnaise
Fresh Asparagus
Ring of Rolls
Royal Chocolate Fingers
Decadent Grapes in White Chocolate

The stage is set for a romantic anniversary picnic. You've chosen the perfect setting, prepared the ultimate menu and are looking forward to an idyllic afternoon in the sunshine. Then down comes the rain! Don't let it spoil a thing. Just move indoors, light the candles and enjoy.

Countdown

Weeks ahead: Make Royal Fingers and freeze.

Several days ahead: Prepare Mayonnaise and Dressing for wild rice, and store in refrigerator.

A day ahead: Cook wild rice, chop ingredients, and toss with salad dressing. Refrigerate. Chill champagne.

On day of serving: Prepare Triple Creme Cheese early in the morning, refrigerate, then bring out to soften at room temperature an hour before guests arrive. Cook lobster, refrigerate; steam asparagus, if serving, and refrigerate. Prepare chocolate-covered grapes and leave in cool place to harden, or refrigerate.

If serving indoors: Substitute Baked Brie for the Triple Creme cheese. Prepare Brie early in the morning, wrap in aluminum foil and keep ready to bake.

If weather cooperates: Pack everything perishable in an iced cooler for transportation to the picnic site. Crack open the lobster for easy eating.

Triple Creme Cheese with Mangoes and Strawberries

Triple Creme cheese is the Rolls Royce of soft cheeses. Try the Brillat-Savarin or the Saint Andre. Decorate the top of the round with slices of fresh mango and strawberries or slice the cheese in half horizontally and make two layers of fruit slices. Serve with plain crackers such as Carr's Table Water Crackers or Melba Toast. I like ANCO Paris Toasts, available at most markets.

Johnny Esaw's Baked Brie

For the past 13 years I have served on the Air Canada Sports Awards Committee and each year on CTV's Wide World of Sports we do a show in Ottawa honouring Canada's outstanding sports executives, coaches and officials. After the show, one of Ottawa's delis puts on a reception. This quick baked cheese appetizer was served at one of the receptions and it was superb! It is so easy to make and looks and tastes a bit like the classic Swiss Fondue. Named for our chairman.   Serves 8 to 10.

- 1 7-inch (18 cms) round of ripe Brie cheese
- 1 ripe mango, peeled and chopped (optional)
- 1 cup (250 mL) sliced strawberries
- Carrs Crackers, Melba Toast or cubes of French bread

Preheat oven to 300 degrees F. (160 degrees C.). With a serrated-edged knife slice off the top "crust" of the Brie. Wrap cheese in foil, place on a cookie sheet and bake for about 20 minutes or until the cheese is soft.

Remove from oven, cut open the top of the foil and slide melted cheese onto a plate, folding the foil around the cheese for support. Place fruit on top of the warm melted cheese and serve. Guests spoon the cheese and fruit onto crackers or bread cubes.

For variety, use Camembert cheese insteads of Brie. Sprinkle either cheese with finely chopped, toasted pistachios, almonds or pecans.

Wild Rice Salad

The queen of rice, combined with hazelnuts and peppers with a ginger chutney dressing, makes a perfect marriage for lobster, considered to be the king of seafoods. Make this dish a day ahead to allow the flavours to mingle. It will keep for several days in the refrigerator.

The dressing also makes an excellent topping for a salad of mixed greens, sesame seeds and citrus fruit sections. Serves 6 to 8.

> 1 cup (250 mL) wild rice
> 2 quarts (2 L) water
> ½ cup (125 mL) toasted hazelnuts, coarsely chopped
> ⅓ cup (80 mL) chopped green onion
> ½ red pepper, chopped finely
> ½ yellow pepper, chopped finely
> ½ cup (125 mL) raisins
> Pinch salt

Wash rice well in strainer, rinsing with cold water for several minutes. Put rice in saucepan with the 2 quarts (2 litres) water, bring to a boil and simmer, uncovered, for 25 to 30 minutes until rice is tender. Don't overcook; the rice grains should be unpopped and still crunchy. Drain well and cool. Toss in a salad bowl with the remaining ingredients, with enough of the dressing to coat well. Cover and refrigerate.

Just before serving, toss with more of the dressing. If you like lots of crunch, don't add the nuts until the very last minute. For variety, use pistachios instead of hazelnuts.

Ginger/Chutney Dressing
> 1 cup (250 mL) salad oil
> 2 tablespoons (30 mL) rice wine vinegar
> Zest and juice of 2 limes
> 3 tablespoons (45 mL) Major Grey's Mango Chutney or other fruit chutney
> 2 tablespoons (30 mL) Chinese candied ginger, finely chopped
> 2 tablespoons (30 mL) candied ginger syrup
> Pepper to taste
> 2 tablespoons (30 mL) soy sauce
> 2 tablespoons (30 mL) honey

Blend well. This can be made several days ahead and kept in the refrigerator.

Cucina Rustica, page 3. Clockwise from top: Bruschetta, Seafood Risotto, Tiramisu, Crostini, Warm Spinach Salad.

Weather Or Not, page 10. Clockwise from top: Camembert Cheese, White Chocolate Grapes, Wild Rice Salad, Royal Chocolate Fingers, Lobster.

Middle East/Moroccan Melange, page 21. Clockwise from top: Moroccan Chicken, Couscous, Moroccan Salad, Meze, Sweets, Tzatziki, Olives, Mint Tea. Photographed at Don & Marcelle McLeans.

Entertaining Santa Fe Style, page 29. Clockwise from top: Chocolate Brownie Torte, Fruit Salsa, Oven Fries, Mustard Dressing, Vegetable Salad Julienne.

Nova Scotia Lobster

*"Consider the lobster, crustacean mobster;
His manners are frightful, but oh, he's delightful."*
                                        Mary Hosford

Lobster is my absolute favourite food, perhaps because I grew up in the Maritimes. I have good memories of lobster feasts. We bought them fresh off the docks for 25 cents a pound when we were at our summer cottage in Shediac, New Brunswick. Today, whenever I visit Halifax, my brother Joel and his wife Ruth always provide a royal lobster feed. We stand around the big steamer pot as Joel stands up each lobster, rubs their backs and sings to them, preferably a Nova Scotian sea shanty. Sounds crazy? Not at all. Maritimers claim that this is the secret for succulence. The lobsters become hypnotized and are therefore totally relaxed when they are dropped into the boiling water. And I have never had lobster anywhere as good as Joel's so it must work. He also adds a bit of sugar to the water to sweeten the pot.

2 to 4 live lobsters, about 1½ lbs (750 g) each

Put enough water in a large pot to totally cover the lobsters and bring to a boil. Drop lobsters into boiling water (whether you stroke them and sing first is up to you) and let them cook for about 15 to 18 minutes, or until they turn red. Fish them out and plunge them briefly into cold water. Alternatively, you might prefer to buy your lobsters pre-cooked, but make sure they are very fresh.

To prepare for serving, either hot or cold, place cooked lobsters on their backs and split lengthwise from head to tail by cutting through the shell and meat with a sharp knife or kitchen shears. Remove dark vein that runs through the body at the centre. Crack large claws. The green liver and red roe are considered delicacies. Try them.

Stock Market's Fresh Chive Mayonnaise

This delicious mayonnaise is hard to beat. It's one of the many fine recipes of Georges and Joanne Lefevbre, owners of Granville Island's Stock Market, one of the most unusual shops to be found anywhere. Here are all the basics, freshly made: soups and stocks, sauces and chutneys, condiments and dressings and many other delectables. And if you get to the market early, then do try their breakfast oatmeal. It's the best!

2 egg yolks
¼ cup (60 mL) finely minced fresh chives
2 tablespoons (30 mL) lemon juice
1 tablespoon (15 mL) Dijon mustard
1 tablespoon (15 mL) minced shallots
1 teaspoon (5 mL) sea salt
1 teaspoon (5 mL) white pepper
1½ cups (375 mL) sunflower oil

Combine all ingredients except the oil in a blender, mixer or food processor and blend well. Add the oil, a few drops at a time while continuing to blend until creamy. Store in the refrigerator for a few days.

Quick Lemon Dill Mayonnaise

Use your favourite bottled mayonnaise and add the seasonings. To each ¾ cup (180 mL) of mayonnaise, blend in ½ teaspoon (2 mL) Dijon mustard, 1 to 2 tablespoons (15 to 30 mL) lemon juice and 1 tablespoon (15 mL) fresh chopped dill. Add pepper to taste. If you can't obtain fresh dill, use 1 teaspoon (5 mL) dried.

Fresh Asparagus

With such a meal, the asparagus is not really necessary, but it does add an extra touch of opulence. Include it if the asparagus is really fresh and you are in the mood. Allow 5 to 6 spears per person, wash them well and steam them for only a few minutes, until they are tender crisp. Drop them into ice water to preserve their fresh green, pat dry and refrigerate. Serve with mayonnaise.

Royal Chocolate Fingers

Once thought to be an aphrodisiac, chocolate is the perfect finale. These concoctions are sinfully rich and should be served in tiny finger morsels. A cheese-cake combination of chocolate, cinnamon and cream cheese sits on a coconut base that will melt in your mouth. The fingers can be made a day or two ahead and kept in the refrigerator and also freeze well. Serve with the chocolate-dipped grapes on the side.

Base
> 1 cup (250 mL) flour
> ¼ cup (60 mL) white sugar
> Pinch salt
> ½ cup (125 mL) butter
> ½ cup (125 mL) finely shredded unsweetened coconut

Filling
> 1 cup (250 mL) softened cream cheese
> 2 squares (2 oz, 56 g) semi-sweet chocolate, melted
> 2 large eggs
> ⅔ cup (160 mL) white sugar
> 2 tablespoon (30 mL) flour
> Pinch salt
> ¾ cup (180 mL) light cream
> 1 teaspoon (5 mL) vanilla
> ½ teaspoon (2 mL) cinnamon

To make the base: Combine flour, sugar and salt and work in the butter until mixture is well blended. Add coconut, cream well together to form a soft ball. Press firmly into a well-greased 8 by 8-inch square (20 by 20 cms) pan.

To make the filling: In mixer or food processor, cream the cheese, melted chocolate, eggs, sugar, flour and salt until fluffy. Add light cream, vanilla and cinnamon, blend well and pour over the prepared coconut base. Bake at 350 degrees F. (180 degrees C.) for about 35 minutes until the top is firm to the touch and filling is set. Check this frequently after about 25 minutes because you don't want to overcook this or it will be dry. Cool, then refrigerate. Slice into tiny fingers.

Decadent Grapes in White Chocolate

Cut off small bunches of washed and dried seedless green grapes and dip into melted white chocolate, turning to coat each grape well. Place on cookie sheet until chocolate hardens. These can be refrigerated or left at room temperature. For 4 to 6 people you will need about 8 oz (225 g) of white chocolate. Belgian chocolate is preferable.

Middle East Moroccan Melange

Turkish Meze
Carrot, Eggplant, Beetroot Salads
Tomato and Pepper Relish
Radishes, olives, Kefalotiri & Quark Cheese
Pita Bread
Tzatziki
Moroccan Roasted Chicken with Almonds and Raisins
Couscous with Chick Peas
Mascarpone Cheese, Stuffed Apricots and Dates
Turkish Delights
Figs, Pistachio Nuts
Mint Tea

Healthy, well-balanced and rich in variety: that's the cuisine of the Middle East and the Balkans. Turkey boasts that its culinary arts rank among the top three in the world (the others being France and China), and having travelled in Turkey recently I can honestly say there is truth to the claim. We found the food always fresh, exciting, different, with lots of fresh fruits, vegetables and seafood. It was also very cheap, if you avoided the big fancy restaurants.

We were fascinated by the markets: huge sacks of spices from around the world, fresh fish from the Black Sea, barbecued right on the boats and stuffed inside fresh bread; whole lamb roasted on vertical spits; food vendors everywhere making fresh sandwiches with meats, tomatoes and cheese topped with Tzatziki. Turkish bread equals France's finest: always fresh from the ovens and rushed to the stores at daybreak.

History books tell us that during the great days of the Ottoman Empire, the Turkish chefs of the imperial kitchens in Topkapi Palace devoted their lives to creating new dishes to please the sultan. With 500 or so concubines and several official and unofficial wives, the Sultan needed to keep up his strength and his chefs laboured round the clock catering to his every whim.

This menu needn't take as long as the Sultan's feasts but it will please and satisfy. In addition to the Turkish delights I have included some of the Moroccan dishes created by my friend Annette Kingery. Don't be alarmed by the length of the menu: everything can be prepared in advance for an easy evening of international tastes.

Countdown

Weeks Ahead: Make Moroccan Chicken and freeze. Make Tomato and Pepper Relish and freeze.

Several days ahead: Prepare Meze Dressing and Tzatziki and refrigerate.

A day ahead: Prepare vegetables, marinate in dressing separately, and refrigerate. Thaw relish. Stew apricots. (If not already frozen, prepare Moroccan Chicken.)

On day of serving: In the morning, stuff apricots and dates; prepare mascarpone cheese mould. Mix Couscous ingredients and cook. An hour before serving, bake chicken and couscous; arrange dessert platter; arrange meze platter and serve with pita.

Meze

Wherever you eat in Turkey you will find a Meze Buffet. Similar to Italian antipasto or Spanish tapas, meze are Turkish appetizers. Several small dishes are served hot or cold, for lunch or dinner, and often as meals in themselves. Greek specialties such as dolmades, squid, spanakopita etc. blend well with the recipes I've included.

If time is a factor, choose a few items from a specialty market to round out your own selection.

Tzatziki

1 large English cucumber, unpeeled, chopped finely
2 cups (500 mL) plain yogurt, strained, or quark
2 cloves garlic, crushed
2 tablespoon (30 mL) chopped green onions
1 teaspoon (5 mL) lemon juice
1 teaspoon (5 mL) white wine vinegar
Pinch pepper
2 teaspoons (10 mL) dried dill weed
½ teaspoon (2 mL) Dijon mustard

Sprinkle cucumber with salt, place in wire strainer and let stand for 10 minutes. Rinse with cold water and pat dry. Add strained yogurt (left overnight in a wire strainer lined with cheesecloth and weighted down with a heavy can) and the rest of the ingredients, adding more or less lemon juice to taste. Refrigerate, covered for 2 to 3 days.

Annette's Vinaigrette Dressing

Annette Kingery has been developing Moroccan recipes for years in her Las Vegas kitchen. Like all good cooks she doesn't need a recipe: she cooks by taste and from the heart. The following are recipes she gave to me after entertaining us royally. They are guide lines only. Use your own judgement by tasting as you go.

¾ cup (180 mL) salad oil
½ cup (125 mL) white wine vinegar
2½ tablespoons (37 mL) cumin
3 cloves garlic, crushed
3 tablespoons (45 mL) Spanish or Hungarian paprika
Salt & pepper to taste

Blend well and store in refrigerator. This can be made several days ahead. Use it for the following Eggplant, Beet and Carrot salads, adding just enough to coat the vegetables.

Eggplant Salad

This salad can be made a day or two ahead. Serves 8 to 12.

3 medium eggplants
8 cloves garlic, peeled
½ teaspoon (2 mL) cumin
1 teaspoon (5 mL) lemon juice

Wash eggplants, make four incisions in each and insert garlic cloves. Bake eggplants on cookie sheet at 450 degrees F. (240 degrees C.) for about 40 minutes or until soft and tender. Peel and mash eggplant pulp, removing most of the seeds as they tend to be bitter. Add cumin and lemon juice. Mix in 3 to 4 tablespoons (45 to 60 mL) of the Vinaigrette Dressing and check seasonings. Refrigerate. To serve, spread on pita or thin slices of French bread.

Beet Salad

Cover 4 lbs (2 kg) fresh beetroot with water, bring to boil and cook until tender. Drain, put into a bowl of cold water and slip off the skins. When cool, cut into uniform slices. Add a few tablespoons of vinaigrette dressing to coat well and refrigerate overnight. This will keep for several days. Toss just before serving, adding more dressing if necessary.

Carrot Salad

Peel and slice 1lb (500 g) of carrots and steam until tender but still firm, about 5 to 8 minutes. Don't overcook: they should still be crisp. Drain and cool. Add enough vinaigrette dressing to coat well and refrigerate for a day or two before serving.

Tomato and Pepper Relish

2 lbs (1 kg) red & green bell peppers
1 tablespoon (15 mL) oil
8 garlic cloves, peeled and finely chopped
2 lbs (1 kg) ripe tomatoes
½ teaspoon (2 mL) salt
2 teaspoons (10 mL) Spanish paprika
¼ teaspoon (1 mL) crushed red pepper flakes
1 cup (250 mL) fresh parsley, chopped

Grill peppers under broiler until skins are black; place in sealed plastic bags until cool enough to handle (they should still be slightly warm). Peel and cut into strips. Heat oil in skillet, add garlic and saute until almost brown. Skin and seed tomatoes, cut into small pieces and add to the skillet. Cover and simmer for 30 minutes. Add pepper strips, paprika, pepper flakes and salt and continue to simmer, uncovered until all liquid has evaporated, stirring occasionally. This will keep for several days in the refrigerator and freezes well. If there is any juice left, strain relish before serving. Makes about 4 cups (1 L). Freeze it in 1 cup (250 mL) containers.

Note: If you find green peppers hard to digest, use all red peppers or a mixture of red and yellow peppers. These are sweeter in flavour.

Moroccan Roasted Chicken
Serves 12.

10 double chicken breasts, boned, skinned and halved
6 medium onions, thinly sliced
1 cup (250 mL) water
¼ cup (60 mL) salad oil
¼ teaspoon (1 mL) dried saffron threads
 dissolved in ¼ cup (60 mL) water
1 teaspoon (5 mL) pepper
Salt to taste
2 teaspoon (10 mL) cinnamon
1 cup (250 mL) raisins or currants
1 cup (250 mL) whole blanched almonds
2 additional teaspoons (10 mL) cinnamon

Cook onions, uncovered, in 1 cup (250 mL) water over medium heat until water is absorbed and onions soft. In a skillet, heat salad oil, add soft onions and saute until golden.

Place chicken breasts in a large bowl. Add saffron, salt, pepper, 2 teaspoons (10 mL) cinnamon and sauteed onions and mix well. Put in a single layer in a large roasting pan. Cover and bake at 400 degrees F. (200 degrees C.) for about 12 minutes; uncover and bake for a further 12 minutes. Add raisins and almonds and sprinkle with the remaining cinnamon. Bake for a further 15 to 20 minutes or until golden brown. Cool, refrigerate.

Before serving, reheat, uncovered, at 350 degrees F. (180 degrees C.) for about 35 minutes or until hot. If chicken starts to dry out, sprinkle with a little chicken stock and cover pan with foil. If necessary, brown finished dish under broiler.

Couscous with Chick Peas

Annette's family recipe for couscous, a marriage of long-simmered onions, chicken, spices and nuts would bring smiles to the sultan himself.

Couscous is a cereal made from coarsely ground durum wheat (semolina). Use the instant variety: it works very well. Add chick peas if desired. When serving, present a bowl filled with hot chicken stock to moisten the dish. Again, this can be made ahead and reheated in a 350 degree F. (180 degree C.) oven for 35 to 40 minutes or until hot. Serves 10 to 12.

3 cups (750 mL) instant couscous
3¼ cups (800 mL) chicken stock
½ cup (125 mL) currants or raisins
1 15-oz (426 mL) can of chick peas, drained
1 teaspoon (5 mL) cinnamon
Pinch saffron or turmeric for colour and flavour (optional)
Salt & pepper to taste
2 to 3 tablespoons (30 to 45 mL) chopped parsley

Bring chicken stock to a boil. In a large saucepan, combine stock with couscous, raisins and chickpeas, spices and seasonings, cover and let stand for about 5 minutes until all liquid has been absorbed. Add parsley just before serving. Serve immediately or cool and refrigerate, reheating when needed.

Apricots and Dates Stuffed with Mascarpone

Middle Eastern desserts often include fresh or dried fruits along with rich, sweet puddings and pastries. In every Turkish restaurant you are served, compliments of the house, the cheese called Mascarpone, the sweet cream cheese of Italy or Quark, pressed yogurt, both of which add interest to fruit such as apricots or dates. For your dinner party include some Turkish Delight candies, figs (to dip in Amaretto liqueur), pistachio or hazelnuts, and glasses of mint tea and your Turkish fantasy will be complete.

> 2 cups (500 mL) whole dried apricots
> 1 cup (250 mL) apricot nectar
> 24 whole dried dates
> 1 cup (250 mL) mascarpone cheese
> 1 cup (250 mL) toasted, finely chopped pistachios

Bring apricot nectar to a boil, Add apricots and simmer for 8 to 10 minutes or until fruit is soft; there should be 2 to 3 tablespoons (30 to 45 mL) of syrup left to glaze the fruit. Cool, and refrigerate.

On the day ahead of serving, split the fruit a little and stuff with enough cheese to fill the centres. Roll tops in pistachios.

Mascarpone and Amaretto

> 1 cup (250 mL) mascarpone cheese
> 4 tablespoons (60 mL) Amaretto liqueur
> Fresh or dried figs, apricots etc.

A few hours before serving, mound the mascarpone cheese on a small plate and make a small hollow in the centre. Refrigerate. Just before serving, transfer cheese to centre of large platter, arrange fruits all around and fill the cheese hollow with the Amaretto liqueur. Guests dip the fruit into the liqueur, and scoop up morsels of the delicious cheese.

Entertaining Santa Fe Style

Vegetable Salad Julienne
French Bread
Crab Cakes or Grilled Chicken Sandwich with Fruit Salsa
and Mustard Dressing
Oven French Fries
Chocolate Brownie Torte

A casual evening of dining with friends for me often includes the ever-popular crab cakes, or a grilled sandwich, Sante Fe style. I serve them with a mid-west fruit salsa and a sharp mustard sauce along with oven fries and a crisp vegetable salad. For dessert, try this triumphant Chocolate Brownie Torte.

Everything on this menu can be prepared in stages to ensure a relaxed and leisurely affair for the chef of the house.

Countdown

Weeks ahead: Make Brownie Torte and freeze.

Several days ahead: Make salad dressing, prepare vegetables, toss together and refrigerate. Make Mustard Dressing.

A day ahead: Bring Brownie Torte to thaw in the refrigerator. Make Fruit Salsa and refrigerate.

On day of serving: In the morning, do the preparation stages for either the chicken sandwich or the crab cakes. Chop the potatoes ready for baking (or pre-cook them now for reheating at the last moment). Just before serving, grill marinated chicken and vegetables for the sandwiches, or finish cooking the crab cakes. Heat bread and toss the salad.

Vegetable Salad Julienne

The southwestern colours of orange, green and yellow make this tangy salad a visual delight. It can be made a least a day or two ahead as it keeps well in the refrigerator. Making julienne strips will be easier if you have a food processor. Serves 6 to 8.

4 large carrots
2 medium zucchini
2 medium size leeks, white parts only
1 head romaine lettuce, separated into leaves

Dressing
¾ cup (180 mL) salad oil
3 tablespoons (45 mL) green onions or shallots, chopped
1 teaspoon (5 mL) Dijon mustard
¼ cup (60 mL) white wine vinegar
1 tablespoon (15 mL) lime or lemon juice (or combination)

Peel carrots, clean zucchini and leeks and slice into very thin julienne strips. Combine salad dressing ingredients and toss with the prepared vegetables. Leave to marinate at least overnight.

To serve, line large platter with romaine lettuce leaves and pile vegetables in the centre.

Crab Cakes

This recipe makes about 8 to 10 little crab cakes to serve 4 people. For 6 to 8 people, you may want to make 1½ times the recipe. The cakes can be made early in the day of serving and then reheated at the last moment. For best results, use fresh crab.

2 eggs, lightly beaten
3 tablespoons (45 mL) mayonnaise
1 cup (250 mL) fine fresh breadcrumbs
2 teaspoons (10 mL) butter
¼ cup (60 mL) shallots or green onion, chopped finely
1 lb (500 g) fresh crabmeat, picked over for shell
1 tablespoon (15 mL) freshly chopped parsley
½ tablespoon (22 mL) Dijon mustard
1 teaspoon (5 mL) lemon juice
Pepper to taste
Dash of Tabasco sauce
½ cup (125 mL) flour
Salt and pepper
2 cups (500 mL) breadcrumbs
2 eggs beaten with 2 tablespoons (30 mL) milk
1 tablespoon (15 mL) salad oil
1 tablespoon (15 mL) butter, melted

Early on the day of serving, lightly beat the eggs, mayonnaise and 1 cup (250 mL) breadcrumbs in a bowl. In a skillet, melt 2 teaspoons (10 mL) butter and saute the shallots or onions for a minute or two. Add onions to the egg mixture, along with crabmeat, parsley, mustard, lemon juice, pepper and Tabasco sauce. Blend well. Chill for about 1 hour.

Form the cooled mixture into 8 to 10 small patties. Mix flour, salt and pepper in a shallow dish and lightly pat each crab cake into the flour mixture to coat. Then dip each into the egg/milk mixture and roll in breadcrumbs. Saute cakes, a few at a time, in the oil and butter, turning once, until golden on both sides. You might have to add a little more butter and oil to the pan.

At this stage, you can either pop them into a 400 degree F. oven (200 degrees C.) to finish cooking for about 10 minutes, or pat dry and refrigerate for reheating later at 350 degrees F. (180 degrees C.) for about 15 minutes or until hot. Either way, serve with some salsa in a radicchio leaf with the mustard dressing on the side.

Quick Crab Cake Sauce

1 4-oz (120 g) can sweet green chilies, drained and chopped
½ cup (125 mL) sour cream
½ cup (125 mL) mayonnaise
1 tablespoon (15 mL) Dijon mustard
Pepper to taste
Dash of Worcestershire sauce

Combine all ingredients and store in the refrigerator

Grilled Chicken Sandwich

One of Vancouver's first and best Southwestern-style restaurants is the Santa Fe Cafe. My choice for lunch is usually their popular Grilled Chicken Sandwich. This is my version, a succulent mixture of chicken and grilled vegetables. It uses recipes from the Halibut Mango Tango menu, on page 58. Serve with the Mustard Dressing or the Stock Market's Fresh Chive Mayonnaise (page 18).

Grilled chicken breasts
Grilled red peppers and Japanese eggplant
Thick slices of sourdough bread

Allow half a pepper and half an eggplant per sandwich. Follow the directions for marinating and grilling the chicken and vegetables given on page 62.

To serve: Brush bread slices with olive oil, place on grill and turn quickly to warm both sides. Put a piece of cooked chicken, pepper and eggplant in each sandwich, spread with Mustard Dressing or the mayonnaise and top with lettuce. How can something so simple taste so good?

Fruit Salsa

This zesty sauce goes well with any grilled fish or chicken.   Serves 4.

½ cup (125 mL) chopped fresh or canned pineapple
½ cup (125 mL) finely chopped mango, fresh or canned
1 red or green chili pepper, seeded, finely chopped
½ cup (125 mL) orange segments, chopped
3 tablespoons (45 mL) finely chopped purple onion
2 teaspoons (10 mL) lime juice
Zest of 1 lime
1 tablespoon (15 mL) each fresh cilantro and mint
Pepper to taste
1 tablespoon (15 mL) raspberry or white wine vinegar
1 tablespoon (15 ml) olive or safflower oil

This is best if made the day ahead of serving, or at least in the morning. Combine all ingredients, cover and store in the refrigerator.

Mustard Dressing

This dressing should also be made at least a day ahead and stored in the refrigerator. It goes particularly well with salmon.

1 tablespoon (15 mL) tomato ketchup
2 tablespoons (30 mL) Dijon mustard
¾ cup (180 mL) sour cream
2 tablespoons (30 mL) plain yogurt
2 tablespoons (30 mL) finely chopped green onions
Couple dashes Tabasco sauce
Pepper to taste
3 tablespoons (45 mL) sweet hamburger pickle relish
Dash of Worcestershire sauce

Combine all ingredients and store in the refrigerator.

Oven French Fries

These are quick, trouble-free and healthy. They are baked in the oven instead of deep-fried. The potatoes can be washed, peeled and cubed ahead of time and kept in ice water. Pat dry and cook just before your guests arrive. (They can also be fully cooked ahead of time and reheated along with the crab cakes.) Serves 6

> 6 medium potatoes
> Salad oil
> ½ to ¾ cup (125 to 180 mL) fresh, finely grated Parmesan cheese
> 4 to 5 garlic cloves, peeled and finely chopped

Peel the potatoes and cut into ½ inch (12 mm) cubes. Keep in ice water. Just before serving, drain potatoes and pat dry. Roll them in a little oil to coat and toss in the Parmesan cheese and garlic. Place on a well-oiled cookie sheet and bake for 25 to 30 minutes at 375 degrees F. (190 degrees C.) or until cooked and golden.

Jack's Chocolate Brownie Torte

Chocolate lovers will devour this—and so will our friend Jack Taunton. Not a brownie and not a cake—it's inbetween and oh so good! Serve it in very small wedges along with coffee ice cream. It freezes very well.
Serves 12.

> 6 oz(170 g) Belgian semi-sweet chocolate
> ½ cup (125 mL) unsalted butter
> ⅓ cup (80 mL) coffee liqueur
> 3 large eggs, separated
> 1 cup (250 mL) fine berry sugar
> 1 teaspoon (5 mL) vanilla
> ⅓ cup (80 mL) flour plus 2 tablespoons (30 mL)
> Pinch salt

In a small saucepan, melt chocolate, butter and liqueur over low heat. Set aside to cool. Beat the egg yolks with sugar and vanilla until mixture is pale and lemon coloured. Add melted chocolate mixture and blend well. Fold in flour and salt, then the egg whites which have been beaten until stiff but not dry.
Butter and flour a 1½-inch (4cm) deep, 8½ inch (20 cm) round baking

pan. Pour mixture in and bake at 350 degrees F. (180 degrees C.) for about 25 to 30 minutes or until it tests done. Cool, remove from pan and glaze.

This can be made a day ahead and stored in the refrigerator, or frozen for several weeks. The cake may also be served unglazed, with strawberries and whipped cream.

Glaze and Garnish
6 oz (170 g) semi-sweet chocolate
½ cup (125 mL) unsalted butter
1 tablespoon (15 mL) light corn syrup
1 tablespoon (15 mL) coffee liqueur
1 cup (250 mL) toasted pecan halves
chopped pecans

Melt chocolate, butter and corn syrup in a saucepan over low heat. Add liqueur. Dip the tips of 10 to 12 toasted pecan halves in the chocolate mixture and set on a cookie sheet to harden. Chop the remaining pecans finely.

Spread glaze over top and sides of the brownie torte. Stand up the chocolate-dipped pecans around the sides and sprinkle the top of the cake with the chopped pecans.

Breakfast of Champions

"The Fitness Group" Smoothie
Frittata Primavera
Bread Basket: Scones, Banana and Poppy Seed Breads
Cornbread, Bagels and Croissants
with
Homemade jams, jellies, cream cheese and Devonshire Cream
Fresh Fruit with Yogurt
Healthy Fruit Trifle

The Vancouver Sun Run is the largest fun run in Canada, drawing over 12,000 joggers and family walkers as well as elite runners. Early on the Sunday morning these keen partipants can be seen running down the main streets of Vancouver and around Stanley Park.

To celebrate this exciting annual event, Barb McQuade, food editor of The Vancouver Sun asked if I could put together a menu for the post-race celebratory breakfast. All of these dishes can be prepared in advance to allow the host or hostess to take part in the run and enjoy their own celebration.

Countdown

Weeks ahead: Make scones, breads etc. and freeze.

A day ahead: Make Frittata Primavera, bake, cool and refrigerate; make custard for trifle, refrigerate.

On the day of serving: Arrange breads in attractive basket with jams and jellies in pretty little dishes. Cover to keep fresh; complete the Fruit Trifle and prepare fruit platter. About 40 minutes before serving, reheat Frittata; whip up Smoothies, heat croissants, bagels etc. Put on the coffee pot.

The Fitness Group Smoothie

One of my pleasures is to start the day off with an exercise class at Barb Crompton's excellent fitness centre, The Fitness Group. After a vigorous workout with instructors Barb, Jo-Ann Stansfield, Julie McNeney and others I am ready for a caffe latte or their own famous fruit drink. Cara Rogers and Jennifer Graveness whip up this magic drink that's full of everything that's good for us. Then I'm full of vim and vigour for the busy day ahead. Makes 1 drink.

½ cup (125 mL) skim milk
½ cup (125 mL) plain yogurt
1 tablespoon (15 mL) wheat bran
1 teaspoon (5 mL) vanilla
1 tablespoon (15 mL) honey
½ ripe banana
1 cup (250 mL) strawberries or blueberries (fresh or frozen)
3 ice cubes (only if fruit is fresh)

Put everything into a blender and whirl at high speed for a few seconds. Try this with other fruit, too, but if you use raspberries you'll want to strain out the seeds.

Frittata Primavera

This hearty frittata is great for weekend brunches and a favourite, too, for apres ski, served with a cup of soup, some hearty grain breads and assorted fruits and cheeses. Add a robust Chianti and you'll feel you're in the Italian Alps. Serves 6.

3 tablespoons (45mL) olive or safflower oil
1 medium Spanish or purple onion, thinly sliced
3 cloves of garlic, crushed finely
3 medium zucchini, chopped into small cubes/(about 2 to 2½ cups (500 to 625 mL)
1 cup (250ml) coarsly chopped fresh mushrooms
1 each small red and yellow peppers, seeded and chopped
Pinch red pepper flakes
6 large eggs, slightly beaten
¼ cup (60 mL) milk, whole or skim
Fresh pepper to taste
2 cups (500 mL) day-old French or wholewheat bread, cubed
8 oz (250 g) light cream cheese, cut into small cubes
2 cups (500 mL) grated Swiss Cheese (Gruyere or Emmenthal)
Topping: fresh ripe tomatoes and Parmesan cheese

Combine first seven ingredients, (oil and all the vegetables) in a large frypan and saute for a few minutes. Drain well.
Combine eggs, milk, pepper, bread cubes and cheeses, then stir in the vegetables. Pour into a greased 10-inch (25cm) springform pan which has been wrapped outside with foil to prevent leaks. Sprinkle top with 2 to 3 tablespoons (30 to 45 mL) of freshly grated Parmesan cheese, put pan on cookie sheet and bake at 350 degrees F. (180 degrees C.) for about 30 to 40 minutes or until golden and firm.
Take briefly from oven and cover top with thin slices of fresh ripe tomatoes and sprinkle with an additional 2 tablespoons (30 mL) of Parmesan cheese. Return to the oven for an additional 5 minutes.

Note: This can be made the day ahead and kept in the refrigerator. Bring it to room temperature, cover well with aluminum foil and reheat, covered with foil, at 350 degrees F. (180 degrees C.) until heated through, about 30 minutes. It can also be reheated in the microwave oven. This dish does not freeze well.

Raisin Scones

It's always fun to provide a variety of breads and biscuits for a brunch like this. These scones are a breakfast staple with my family. They're quick to make and are best served warm with jam, cream cheese or Devonshire cream. They freeze well. Makes about 10.

2½ cups (625 mL) flour
1 tablespoon (15 mL) baking powder
½ teaspoon (2 mL) baking soda
2 tablespoons (30 mL) white sugar
¼ teaspoon (1 mL) salt
½ cup (125 mL) cold unsalted butter, cut into bits
½ cup (125 mL) raisins
1 cup (250 mL) buttermilk or sour milk
1 egg
Egg wash
1 egg, 1 tablespoon (15 mL) milk, beaten
Sweet Topping (optional)
½ cup (125 mL) toasted sliced almonds
2 tablespoons (30 mL) berry sugar

In a bowl combine flour, baking powder, baking soda, sugar and salt. Cut in the butter until well blended and add the raisins. In a separate bowl combine eggs and milk and beat well. Add all at once to flour mixture, stirring lightly to form a ball.

Turn dough out onto a floured surface, knead gently to form a smooth, soft dough. Roll out into a circle about ¾ inch (18 mm) thick. Cut into small rounds (about 2½ inches (7 cm) in diameter) and place on cookie sheet. Brush tops with egg wash and sprinkle with topping. Bake at 400 degrees C. (200 degrees C.) for about 15 minutes or until baked through and golden.

Margaret Rogers' Banana Bread

Margaret attended my early Cooking School classes and also held classes of her own. Her simple recipe for banana bread is well described by the note on the recipe she gave to me: "The best banana bread I've ever tasted. Very moist." I totally agree. Thanks, Margaret for this great classic! The bread freezes well so make several to tuck away. Makes 1 loaf.

2 large bananas, very ripe, almost black
1 teaspoon (5 mL) baking soda
5 tablespoons (75 mL) milk
½ cup (125 mL) butter
1 cup (250 mL) white sugar
1 egg
1 teaspoon vanilla
1⅓ cup (330 mL) all purpose flour
1 teaspoon (5 mL) baking powder

This recipe is made in four easy stages. First mash together the bananas, baking soda and milk and leave to stand. Then blend the butter with the sugar, egg and vanilla. Sift together the flour and baking powder and finally mix everything together, just enough to blend. Don't overdo it.

Pour mixture into a greased loaf pan and bake at 350 degrees F. (180 degrees C.) for 50 to 60 minutes or until tested clean with a skewer or straw. Cool. Wrap in foil, then plastic wrap. It is best eaten the following day and is great toasted.

Poppyseed Loaf

This quick-as-a-wink recipe originated in the Kootenays in the little mining town of Wilmer (it's near Invermere) where Dorothea Dean runs a great little bed and breakfast establishment in a restored turn-of-the-century hotel, Delphine Lodge. I've cut down on the oil and added a little nip of lemon.　　　　　　　　　　　　　　　Makes 1 loaf.

¾ cup (180 mL) sunflower oil
1 cup (250 mL) white sugar
2 large eggs
2 cups (500 mL) flour
4 teaspoons (20 mL) baking powder
1 cup (250 mL) 2 % evaporated milk
1 cup (250 mL) poppy seeds
½ teaspoon (2 mL) grated lemon zest

Put all ingredients into bowl, in any order, and mix well. Pour into greased loaf pan and bake for about an hour at 350 degrees F. (180 degrees C.)

Note: If you don't like the crunch of poppy seeds, soften them in the milk for 5 to 10 minutes.

Healthy Fruit Trifle

The culinary highlight of the 1990 Commonwealth Games food concession at the Athletic Stadium in Auckland, New Zealand was the special fruit cup. It was simple, a triple-layered concoction of creamy custard, fruit and yogurt or whipped cream, served icy cold in tall plastic cups, but it was so good! My favourite flavour was apricot, but fresh strawberries came a close second. This is my version, using a packaged custard mix for speed. Serves 4 to 5.

1 package Jello Vanilla Pudding Mix (not instant)
1 tablespoon (15 mL) cornstarch
3 cups (750 mL) milk
1 tablespoon (15 mL) butter
About 2 cups (500 mL) fresh fruit, chopped
Plain or vanilla yogurt, or whipped cream

Make pudding mix according to package directions, but adding cornstarch to dry mix and using an extra cup of milk. (The cornstarch and extra milk make the pudding less sweet and creamier.) When cooked, swirl in the butter. Cover and leave to cool, then divide between 4 or 5 tall glasses or wine goblets. Chill. Shortly before serving, cut up fresh fruit and cover custard with a thick layer. Top with several spoonfuls of whipped cream, yogurt or creme fraiche and refrigerate. Mmmm, good!

The Big Production

Champagne
Smoked Salmon
Warm Wild Mushroom Salad
Pecan Cheese Crisps
Roast Pheasant or Rock Cornish Game Hens with Wild Rice
Asparagus with Lemon Butter Sauce
Chocolate Ganache Torte
with Orange Glaze

Will this elegant, impressive menu take forever to prepare? The answer is "No!" But to bring it off successfully, you definitely need good planning. Everything on the menu can be prepared in stages well ahead of time, leaving only last minute touches to complete.

Haik Gharibian, noted for his imaginative parties, created a centrepiece that sets the mood for festivity: plump pheasants decked out in all their splendour. Start the party off in grand style with champagne and smoked salmon. Serve the following courses leisurely, allowing time to savour each one.

Countdown

Weeks ahead: Make Pecan Cheese Crisps and Chocolate Ganache Torte and freeze.

Days Ahead: Make Orange Glaze and Vinaigrette Dressing and refrigerate. Prepare salad greens and refrigerate in plastic bags.

A Day ahead: Make Yam Croutons; prepare Wild Rice Stuffing and refrigerate; make Butter Sauce for asparagus and thaw Torte in refrigerator.

On Day of serving: In the morning, take Cheese Crisps from freezer; stuff birds and refrigerate; prepare salmon platter, wrap and refrigerate. Start cooking the birds an hour or so before guests arrive (earlier if you are serving pheasants); reheat salad dressing and croutons. Finish preparations for salad just before serving. Wait to steam the asparagus until the very last minute.

Warm Wild Mushroom Salad

The smoky taste of wild mushrooms and bacon, topped with yam croutons and hazelnuts make this salad unusual. Its interesting flavours are accented by a warm vinaigrette dressing. If wild mushrooms are unobtainable, use regular mushrooms.   Serves 8.

5 to 6 heads assorted salad greens
   (romaine, purple leaf, butter lettuce, etc.)
2 cups (500 mL) wild mushrooms (oyster, shiitake, chanterelles, etc.)
2 cups (500 mL) yam croutons (recipe follows)
1 cup (500 mL) toasted chopped hazelnuts

Vinaigrette Dressing

½ lb (250 g) bacon
2 tablespoons (30 mL) bacon fat
2 cloves garlic, finely chopped
½ cup (125 mL) shallots, chopped
¼ cup (60 mL) green onions, chopped
⅓ cup (80 mL) champagne or white wine vinegar
1 cup (250 mL) peanut or safflower oil
Pepper to taste

Make the dressing a day or two ahead of serving: Fry bacon in heavy skillet; drain, chop and refrigerate. In the same skillet, heat 2 tablespoons (30 mL) of the bacon fat and saute the garlic, shallots and onions for a few minutes. Add vinegar, oil and pepper, cool and refrigerate.

Clean, dry, and stem the mushrooms (shiitake stems are tough, good only for soup); refrigerate.

Just before serving: Slice mushrooms thinly and saute in 1 tablespoon (15 mL) of oil plus 1 teaspoon (5 mL) butter, cooking only until tender. Add the cooked bacon bits, sprinkle with pepper, add the prepared dressing and keep warm.

Reheat yam croutons on a cookie sheet in a 350 degree F. (180 degree C.) oven for 5 to 8 minutes until heated through. Watch that they don't become too brown.

To serve: In a large salad bowl break up the greens and mix, then add the warm mushroom/salad dressing very slowly, then toss gently. Add more pepper if desired. Divide among 8 serving plates, sprinkle each with a few yam croutons and hazelnuts. Serve immediately.

Yam Croutons

These can be made a day ahead and crisped in the oven just before serving.

> 3 medium-sized yams or sweet potatoes
> Olive or salad oil

Peel and slice the yams and cut into tiny cubes. Toss with enough oil to coat and place on well-greased cookie sheet. Bake at 375 degrees F. (190 degrees C.) for about 20 minutes or until crisp on the outside, soft on the inside, Toss once or twice while they are baking. Cool, store in refrigerator.

Reheat at 350 degrees F. (180 degrees C.) for 5 to 8 minutes just before serving.

Pecan Cheese Crisps

These crispy little appetizers are ideal to serve with cold beer or wine. They can be made days ahead of time to keep on hand in the cookie jar, and they also freeze well. You can vary the flavour by changing the type of cheese used—try Monterey Jack, mozzarella or blue.

> 1 cup (250 mL) sharp Cheddar cheese, grated
> 2 tablespoons (30 mL) soft butter
> ½ cup (125 mL) flour
> ½ teaspoon (2 mL) Hungarian or Spanish sweet paprika
> Pinch salt
> ¼ cup (60 mL) milk
> ½ cup (125mL) finely chopped toasted pecans

Blend cheese and butter in a mixing bowl. Add flour, paprika and salt, then add milk and mix well to form a soft dough. Fold in pecans. Take small pieces of dough (about ½ teaspoon/2 mL) and place well apart on a large greased cookie sheet. Spread dough pieces as flat as you can, using the back of a spoon. They will spread while they bake, so leave plenty of room between them.

Bake at 400 degrees F. (200 degrees C.) for 8 to 10 minutes or until the edges start to turn golden brown. Cool on wire racks. These zesty morsels will keep for a week or so in an airtight container, or they can be frozen for longer storage. Serve at room temperature or reheat at 350 degrees F. (180 degrees C.) for about 5 minutes to serve hot.

Roast Pheasant or Rock Cornish Game Hens

Order the pheasants from your butcher or meat department well ahead of time. They are not always available. But Rock Cornish game hens make perfectly acceptable substitutes. A pheasant will usually serve 2, a game hen 1 to 2, depending on size. Serves 8.

4 pheasants or 4 or 8 game hens, depending on size
4 cups (1 L) cooked wild rice (recipe follows)
4 tablespoons (60 mL) olive or safflower oil
4 tablespoons (60 mL) brandy
Apricot jam, melted

Blend oil and brandy to use as basting sauce. Clean the birds, sprinkle cavities with pepper and a little salt and fill each with about ¾ cup (180 mL) cooked wild rice (less for game hens, particularly if they are small.) Truss birds for roasting then place on oiled racks in roasting pans and bake at 400 degrees F. (200 degrees C.) for about 2½ hours (1 hour for game hens) until the legs are tender, basting frequently with the brandy-oil mixture. During the final 15 minutes of roasting, baste with the apricot jam.

Cover the cooked birds and keep warm until ready to serve on a large platter garnished with parsley, watercress, kumquats or orange slices.

Skim the fat from the juices in the roasting pan and transfer juices to a small skillet. Add a little dry white wine, then slowly whisk in 2 tablespoons (30 mL) of butter. Pour this glaze over the birds just before serving.

Wild Rice Stuffing

The stuffing can be cooked the day ahead of serving but don't stuff the birds until the following morning, then refrigerate until ready to roast.

Makes 4 cups, enough for 8 people.

2 tablespoons (30 mL) butter
1 cup (250 mL) water chestnuts, chopped
⅓ cup (80 mL) white onions, chopped
2 cups (500 mL) raw wild rice
4 cups (1 L) chicken stock
3 tablespoons (45 mL) finely chopped parsley
Pinch thyme
Salt & pepper

Melt butter in a large saucepan and briefly saute the water-chestnuts and onions. Add rice and stir together for a few minutes, then add stock, parsley and seasonings. Bring to a boil and simmer for 35 to 45 minutes or until all the stock is absorbed. Cool, then refrigerate.

Asparagus with Lemon Butter Sauce

As soon as the robins begin to sing in the spring, then you can expect fresh asparagus to appear in the markets. (For a pleasant change, try the delicate white asparagus, when you can find it.) Treat the tender spears gently: only a very light steaming is necessary. Allow 5 to 6 stalks per person. Break off only a short piece from the base of each and peel the bottom half of the stalk with a potato peeler for a two-toned effect.

Sauce

4 to 5 tablespoons (60 to 75 mL) salted butter
1 garlic clove, crushed
Juice of 1 to 1½ lemons
Pepper to taste

The butter sauce can be made the day ahead. In a small saucepan heat the butter until frothy. Add garlic and lightly saute. Add lemon juice and pepper to taste. Cool, then refrigerate

On the day of serving, reheat the sauce to warm. Wash and peel the asparagus. At the last possible moment, steam lightly for just a few minutes, drain, pour over the warm sauce and serve immediately.

Fresh Chef 47

Chocolate Ganache Torte

A dark, delicious and very rich dessert, this can be made several days ahead and kept in the freezer. Thaw overnight or early on the morning of serving and serve with Orange Glaze.   Serves 12 to 16.

Base Crust
> 1 cup (250 mL) finely chopped toasted almonds or hazelnuts
> ¼ cup (60 mL) unsalted butter, melted
> ¼ cup (60 mL) white sugar

Filling
> 1 lb (450 g) Belgian semi-sweet chocolate
> 4 tablespoons (90 mL) unsalted butter
> 1 egg yolk, slightly beaten
> 2 tablespoons (30 mL) orange liqueur or orange concentrate
> 2 tablespoons (30 mL) icing sugar
> 3 cups (750 mL) whipping cream, whipped

Crust: Blend nuts with melted butter and sugar and press in the bottom of a 9 to 10-inch (18 to 22 cm) springform pan. Bake for 10 to 12 minutes at 350 degrees F. (180 degrees F.) until golden and firm. Cool and set aside.

Filling: Melt chocolate and butter over low heat in a heavy saucepan. Whip in the beaten egg yolk, liqueur and icing sugar and cool slightly. Gently fold in the whipped cream and pour into cooled crust. Cover and refrigerate, at least overnight, or freeze.

Orange Glaze
> Zest of 3 oranges, chopped finely
> 1 cup (250 mL) fresh orange juice
> ¾ cup (180 mL) white sugar
> 3 tablespoons orange liqueur

Put all ingredients except the liqueur into a small, heavy saucepan, bring to a boil, then reduce heat and cook until sauce starts to thicken, about 10 minutes. It should be the consistency of medium syrup. Cool slightly, then add liqueur. Reheat to warm just before serving.

This sauce will keep for several weeks in the refrigerator and it is wonderful on vanilla, chocolate or coffee ice cream.

To serve Ganache: Place small wedges of ganache cake on to individual serving plates and pour over a little orange glaze. Decorate with fresh berries or a baby rose.

The Big Production, page 43. Clockwise from top: Wild Mushroom Salad, Pheasant, Wild Rice, Asparagus, Chocolate Ganache Torte. Photographed at Haik Gharibians.

Portable Pleasures, page 53. Clockwise from top: Coconut Meringue Cake, Rice Krispy Chocolate Chips, Moroccan Vegetable Salad, Greek Lemon Chicken, Pesto Potato Salad.

Halibut Mango Tango, page 58. Clockwise from top: Grilled Halibut & Grilled Vegetables, Thai Rice, Artichokes & Lemon Butter Sauce, Rolls, Tarte Au Citron. Photographed at Don & Marcelle McLeans.

Portable Pleasures

Greek Lemon Chicken
Moroccan Vegetable Salad
Pesto Potato Salad
Baguette Bread
Dianne's Rice Krispies Chocolate Chip Cookies
Ruth's Coconut Meringue Cake
Fresh Fruit Trio

Summer entertaining on a boat, at the summer cottage or campsite requires food that can be easily transported and hearty enough to satisfy an outdoor appetite. Here the traditional picnic fare of chicken and potato salad gets a new twist, livened up with zesty spices and herbs and leaning on the culinary traditions of Italy, Morocco and Greece. But to keep the family heritage alive, I've added good old chocolate chip cookies and coconut cake, along with fresh fruit for a well-rounded informal meal.

Countdown

Weeks ahead: Make Coconut Meringue Cake and freeze. Prepare Greek Lemon Chicken and freeze.

Several days ahead: Make dressing for Moroccan Salad.

A day ahead: Prepare vegetables for Moroccan Salad, toss with dressing and refrigerate. Cook potatoes and complete salad, tossing with pesto to coat well. Make Chocolate Chip Cookies and keep fresh in sealed container.

On day of picnic: Pack all perishables in well-iced coolers and don't let them sit too long in the sun when serving. Pack other dishes in strong plastic containers, preferably those that can double as serving dishes.

Greek Lemon Chicken

Definitely for lemon lovers, this dish is tart, tender and moist. It can be made a day ahead and served cold or hot. Serves 8.

4 whole chicken breasts, divided, and/or 8 whole legs
Marinade
3 tablespoons (45 mL) olive oil
½ cup (125 mL) lemon juice
Zest of 3 lemons
1½ teaspoons (7 mL) each dried thyme and rosemary
4 cloves garlic, crushed
Pepper to taste

Skin and bone the chicken breasts, skin the chicken legs and cut into drumsticks and thighs. Place chicken in a single layer in a large shallow casserole dish and cover with the marinade, made by combining all the ingredients. Leave in marinade for 3 to 4 hours in the refrigerator.
    Heat oven to 350 degrees F. (180 degrees C.). Remove chicken from marinade. Cook drumsticks and thighs for 30 minutes, then add chicken breasts and continue to cook for about 20 minutes more until meat is no longer pink, but still moist. If necessary, place cooked chicken under broiler to brown slightly. Save juices to reheat later and glaze the chicken before transporting. Serve on a bed of lettuce decorated with slices of lemon.

Pesto Potato Salad

When the tiny summer potatoes and green beans are at their sweetest, cook them gently and toss with your favourite homemade or deli pesto. The taste is sensational! Make the salad a day or two ahead for best flavour and serve hot or cold. Serves 8 to 12.

8 cups (2 L) baby new potatoes, red or white
3 cups (750 mL) fresh green beans, sliced diagonally
1 small purple onion, chopped finely (about 1 cup, 250 mL)
½ cup (125 mL) thinly sliced radishes
½ cup (125 mL) pesto
Salt and pepper to taste.

Cut potatoes into halves or quarters, cover with cold water and boil gently until they are just tender, about 10 to 15 minutes. Steam beans for 8 to 10 minutes. Drain and cool the vegetables.

Toss potatoes, beans, radishes and chopped onion in a large salad bowl. Sprinkle with salt and pepper and toss again with the pesto to coat well. Cover and refrigerate.

To serve the salad hot, turn into a skillet and stir over medium heat until heated through. Serve with a sprinkle of grated Parmesan cheese.

Moroccan Vegetable Salad

This recipe is one that I have used for 15 years and it is still a favourite, redolent with Middle Eastern spices. It's great with barbecued lamb and salmon. It can be made a day ahead and refrigerated.

Serves 10 to 12.

4 cups (1 L) small mushrooms, halved
4 cups (1 L) cherry tomatoes
1 can (19 oz, 540 mL) garbanzo beans or chick peas, drained
1 cup (250 mL) large black olives, halved
2 cups (500 mL) celery, sliced on the diagonal
1 each red, green and orange pepper, thinly sliced
1 cup (250 mL) finely chopped purple or green onions
Lettuce greens

Dressing
¾ cup (180 mL) plain yogurt
½ cup (125 mL) mayonnaise
2 tablespoons (30 mL) olive oil
1 tablespoon (15 mL) lemon juice
2 cloves garlic, crushed
Pepper to taste
¾ teaspoon (3 mL) cumin
1/8 teaspoon (.5 mL) turmeric
3 tablespoons (45 mL) fresh dill or 1½ teaspoons (7 mL) dried dill

Combine all dressing ingredients and store in a covered container in the refrigerator. On the day ahead, toss the vegetables in a large salad bowl and add enough dressing to coat. Refrigerate, covered, overnight. Trim the salad bowl at the last moment with a few leafy greens. The salad is great with pita bread for a hearty (and healthy) snack.

Dianne's Rice Krispies Chocolate Chip Cookies

My sister-in-law Dianne Matheson always has a new recipe for me to try on my Toronto jaunts. Knowing that I crave chocolate, she surprised me last time with these cookies, an old favourite spruced up with the addition of Rice Krispies. No, they won't snap, crackle or pop but they will go down well. Kids will love them. Makes about 4 dozen.

1½ cups (375 mL) soft butter
¾ cup (180 mL) white sugar
1 cup (250 mL) brown sugar
2 large eggs
1 teaspoon (5 mL) vanilla
1½ cups (375 mL) all purpose flour
½ teaspoon (3 mL) baking powder
1 teaspoon (5 mL) baking soda
1 teaspoon (5 mL) salt
2 cups (500 mL) Rice Krispies
2 cups (500 mL) Quick (not instant) Quaker Oats
1 cup (250 mL) semi-sweet chocolate chips

Combine butter, sugar, eggs and vanilla and cream well. Mix together the flour, baking powder, baking soda and salt and add to the butter mixture, mixing until just blended. Mix Rice Krispies, oats and chocolate chips together and add to the mixture. Stir well. The batter will be soft.

Drop batter a tablespoon (15 mL) at a time onto a greased cookie sheet, leaving about 2 inches (5 cms) between cookies. Press down cookies slightly with the back of a spoon. Bake for 7 to 8 minutes at 375 degrees F. (190 degrees C.) until golden. Transfer to wire rack to cool and store in air-tight containers.

Ruth's Coconut Meringue Cake

My other sister-in-law Ruth Matheson from Halifax is a renowned artist and teacher and also a marvellous cook. Her coconut meringue cake is an old family recipe that just seems to get better every year.

>½ cup (125 mL) white sugar
>¼ cup (60 mL) butter
>6 tablespoons (90 mL) milk
>3 egg yolks
>1 cup (250 mL) all purpose flour
>1 teaspoon (5 mL) baking powder
>Pinch salt
>
>**Topping**
>>3 egg whites
>>½ cup (125 mL) white sugar
>>1 teaspoon (5 mL) vanilla
>>1 cup (250 mL) shredded coconut

To make the cake: Cream butter and sugar until light, then beat in the egg yolks. Add milk. Fold in flour, baking powder and salt and beat just until smooth. Pour into a greased 8 by 8 inch (20 cms) square pan.

To make the topping: Beat egg whites until thick. Add sugar a spoonful at a time, continuing to beat until sugar is dissolved. Fold in vanilla and coconut. Spread topping evenly on top of cake batter and bake at 350 degrees F. (180 degrees C.) for about 30 minutes or until the cake tests done. Cool. Store in airtight container and cut into squares to serve. The cake freezes well.

Halibut Mango Tango

Fresh California Artichokes with Lemon Butter Sauce
Grilled Halibut with Mango/Lime Puree
or
Grilled Chicken with Red Pepper/Tomato Chutney
Grilled Vegetables
Thai Rice in Coconut Milk
Tarte au Citron

The Halibut Mango Tango may not be as exhausting as the Lambada, but food aficionados will find it every bit as exciting. It's an easy-to-prepare meal to be enjoyed when fresh halibut is at its peak. When halibut is not available, substitute other fish or the chicken for an equally titillating taste. Grilled vegetables are interesting and easy and fresh artichokes make a dramatic start. The tart lemon pie is one of my classic desserts—a popular choice for any occasion.

I owe the title for this meal to my daughter's friend Ellen Cohen from Montreal. She liked the fish dish so much, she christened it.

Countdown

Weeks ahead: Make Tarte au Citron and freeze.

Several days ahead: Make Creme Fraiche and keep in refrigerator. Toast sesame seeds.

A day ahead: Make Lemon Butter Sauce and Marinade for fish and vegetables.

On day of serving: In the morning defrost dessert; prepare artichokes and Mango-Lime Sauce; marinate fish and vegetables. (If serving chicken, prepare marinade and steep chicken; make Red Pepper/Tomato Chutney.) Thirty minutes before serving, heat grill; cook rice and keep warm; heat butter sauce for artichokes and steam artichokes; put fish or chicken and vegetables on grill.

California Artichokes

When spring rolls around, California sends us one of its great delicacies: artichokes. They are low in calories, about 25 per edible portion, and contain significant amounts of Vitamin C. Cook the artichokes (which are in reality members of the thistle family) then dip each tender petal in a light lemon-butter sauce for a special treat.

To prepare and serve artichokes:
The following advice comes from the California Artichoke Advisory Board. April and May are the months when artichokes are most plentiful. Allow one whole artichoke per person, choosing those of equal size for even cooking. If the petals are tipped with bronze, (known as "winter-kissed") the insides should be extra flavourful.

Pull off the lower petals and cut stems to one inch (2.5 cm) or less. Cut off top quarter of artichoke and if desired, snip tips off petals. Boil artichokes, standing them in three inches (8 cm) of boiling, salted water. Cover and simmer for 25 to 40 minutes depending on size, or until one of the central petals pulls out easily. Stand upside down to drain.

Serve them hot or cold. Pull off outer petals one at a time, dip base of petal into lemon-butter sauce and pull through teeth to remove soft inside. Discard outer skin. When all petals have been removed, spoon out the fuzzy centre at the base and discard. The bottom of the artichoke, known as the heart, is delicious. Cut into small pieces and dip into the sauce.

Lemon Butter Sauce
Serves 6.

Juice of 4 lemons
5 tablespoons (75 mL) melted butter
2 tablespoons (30 mL) green onion, finely chopped
Salt & pepper to taste
½ cup (125 mL) toasted sliced almonds

On the day ahead of serving, combine all ingredients except the almonds; blend well and refrigerate. To serve, reheat gently, and add almonds. To serve, place cooked artichokes on individual plates and pass hot sauce.

Grilled Halibut

The delicate taste of freshly-caught halibut is accented by a tangy mango/lime sauce. The fish is first steeped in a Japanese marinade, which is also used for the grilled vegetables.   Serves 6.

6 6-oz (180 g) pieces of halibut, boned and skinned
Japanese Marinade
   6 tablespoons (90 mL) sake or sherry
   6 tablespoons (90 mL) soy sauce
   3 tablespoons (45 mL) sesame oil

Mix all ingredients and divide into two portions, one for the halibut, the other for the vegetables. Marinate the halibut for 2 to 3 hours, turning once in a while. Have barbecue coals as hot as possible, oil the grill well and grill the fish, allowing about 5 minutes for each ½ inch (13 mm) of thickness, measured at the thickest part. Take care not to overcook. The fish should be ready when it is no longer translucent. About 4 to 5 minutes per side should be enough. Serve with the sauce.

Mango/Lime Sauce

2 to 3 peeled and sliced mangoes, about 2 cups (500 mL)
   or 1 14 oz (398 mL) can sliced mangoes
1 tablespoon (15 mL) fresh ginger, finely chopped
½ cup (125 mL) chicken stock
2 tablespoons (30 mL) lime juice
Chopped zest of 1 lime
1 tablespoon (15 mL) fresh orange juice
2 tablespoons (30 mL) chopped fresh basil
   or ½ teaspoon (2 mL) dried basil

This sauce can be made the day ahead of serving. Combine all ingredients in a food processor (or chop and blend thoroughly.) Heat through just before serving, thinning out with stock if mixture is too thick. Add more basil to taste. To serve: put a little of the sauce on a plate and top with the grilled halibut. Add vegetables and rice.

Grilled Chicken with Red Pepper Chutney

This recipe is my adaptation of the dish served to food enthusiasts at Vancouver's Four Seasons, where both the Four Seasons' chef and the chef from California's Mondavi Winery shared their creations with us.

Serves 6.

6 whole chicken breasts, boned, skinned, halved
California Marinade
½ cup (125 mL) lemon juice
1 tablespoon (15 mL) finely chopped lemon zest
2 tablespoons (30 mL) Dijon mustard
¼ cup (60 mL) mixed herbs (fresh rosemary, thyme, basil, oregano and parsley)
Coarsely cracked pepper

Combine marinade ingredients and pour over single layer of chicken breasts in a glass dish. Cover and refrigerate for 2 to 4 hours. Grill the chicken breasts for 6 to 8 minutes on each side and serve with a spoonful of chutney.

Red Pepper Chutney

Great for all grilled fish and meats.

4 large tomatoes, peeled, seeded and chopped
3 red peppers, grilled, peeled and chopped
6 tablespoons (90 mL) raspberry vinegar
4 tablespoons (60 mL) white sugar

In a small skillet, mix the vinegar and sugar and cook until it starts to form a thin syrup and the sugar begins to caramelize. Add to well drained tomatoes and red peppers, stir to blend and heat through. This is best made on the day of serving.

Grilled Vegetables

3 baby Japanese eggplants, split in half
2 red peppers, cored and halved
About 25 to 30 snowpeas (allow 2 to 3 per person)
6 large fresh shiitake or regular mushrooms, stemmed

Blanch snowpeas in boiling water for about 30 seconds, pat dry. Marinate all the vegetables in the reserved Japanese marinade for about 30 minutes. Grill for a few minutes on each side until tender, brushing freqiently with marinade. The vegetables can be cooked the same time as the fish, if there is room on the grill. The blackened skin of the peppers can be peeled off, and the peppers cut into strips for serving.

Note: Zucchini also grills well and cooks in the same amount of time as eggplant. Cut them lengthwise. Purple onions, cut into halves, are another good addition.

Thai Rice with Coconut Milk

Usually found in Oriental markets, Thai rice is slightly sticky when cooked. If you can't find it, then use Chinese long-grained white rice. The canned coconut milk will give it a creamy, subtle flavour. For garnish, I used black sesame seeds but plain sesame seeds, toasted to a golden brown, will do as well. Serves 6 to 8.

2 cups raw Thai rice
2 cups water
2 cups canned coconut milk
Sesame seeds, black or toasted

In a saucepan, bring water and coconut milk to the boil. Add rice, stir. Cover pot and simmer for about 20 minutes or until liquid has been absorbed. Stir well to blend. For serving, shape rice into squares (being slightly sticky it moulds easily) and top each serving with sesame seeds.

Tarte au Citron

This is great any time of year—I sometimes make it at Christmas for a fresh change of pace. The feather-light lemon filling is accented by the crunch of toasted almonds. Serve in thin slices, garnished if desired with fresh berries. The tarte can be made ahead because it freezes very well. Serves 8.

Pastry
> 1 cup (250 mL) flour
> ¼ cup (60 mL) sugar
> ⅓ cup (80 mL) butter
> 1 egg, slightly beaten

Combine flour and sugar and cut in butter until mixture resembles coarse meal. Stir in egg, mixing well. Wrap and chill for 30 minutes, then roll out to line a 9-inch (22 cm) flan pan with removable sides. Press pastry well into bottom and up sides and prick with fork. Bake at 375 degrees F. (190 degrees C.) for 8 minutes. Cool. The pastry shell can be made a couple of days ahead of serving, unless you choose to make the complete dish ahead and freeze it.

Filling
> 3 eggs
> ½ cup (125 mL) sugar
> Juice of 3 lemons
> Chopped zest of 3 lemons
> ¾ cup (180 mL) finely ground almonds
> ½ cup (125 mL) melted butter, cooled
> ½ cup (125 mL) sliced almonds, toasted

Whisk together eggs, sugar, lemon juice, rind and ground almonds. Add melted and cooled butter and pour into pastry shell. Bake at 375 degrees F. (190 degrees C.) for 25 to 30 minutes. Garnish with toasted sliced almonds and a dollop of Creme Fraiche.

Creme Fraiche
> 1 cup (250 mL) whipping cream
> 1 cup (250 mL) sour cream

Combine ingredients and leave, covered, at room temperature for 24 hours. Cover and refrigerate for at least a week.

Shades of Summer

Avocado Oriental Salad
with Cantonese Dressing
Grilled Tiger Prawns with Limes
Grilled Vegetables (Optional)
Sourdough Baguette Bread
Strawberries with Champagne Zabaglione

Grilled seafood evokes memories of a recent trip to the Greek island of Rhodes. Wandering through the Old Town we settled for dinner at a quaint, romantic garden restaurant where they served grilled prawns and snapper, fresh from the sea.

This menu is perfect for an informal patio luncheon or dinner. Just put the salad platter, the grilled vegetables (recipe on page 62), the bread and prawns on the table and let everyone help themselves. The salad dressing doubles as a dip for the prawns and the vegetables. You'll need to provide finger bowls and plenty of napkins as the guests peel their own prawns.

The dessert is light and heavenly: fresh strawberries or other berries with a light-as-a-cloud zabaglione custard made with champagne.

Countdown

Several days ahead: Make salad dressing and refrigerate; clean and dry lettuce and endive and store in plastic bags in refrigerator.

On day of serving: In the morning, clean and rinse prawns but leave in shells; slice hearts of palm, mango and melon and refrigerate. Prepare marinade and steep vegetables for grilling (see page 62); clean strawberries. Just before guests arrive, warm bread in oven; heat grill for grilling prawns and vegetables; arrange salad ingredients on platter and toss with dressing. Place strawberries in wine goblets and assemble ingredients for the zabaglione.

Avocado Oriental Salad

The Cantonese Dressing is also excellent as a dipping sauce for grilled vegetables, meats or seafoods.   Serves 8

2 heads butter lettuce, cleaned & dried
4 ripe avocados, peeled, cut in half (do this at the very last moment)
1 14-oz can (398 mL) hearts of palm, drained, thinly sliced
2 ripe mangos, peeled and sliced or 14-oz can (398 mL) canned mango
1 honeydew melon, peeled and sliced
2 Belgian endive, cleaned, dried, separated into leaves

Cantonese Dressing
1 cup (250 mL) mayonnaise
½ cup (125 mL) plain yogurt
4 tablespoons (60 mL) peanut oil or salad oil
3 tablespoons (45 mL) soy sauce
2 cloves garlic, crushed
3 tablespoons (45 mL) chopped shallots
Dash of Tabasco sauce
1 tablespoon (15 mL) lemon juice
Zest of 1 lemon
1 tablespoon (15 mL) each of fresh basil, oregano, tarragon, thyme
   or 1 teaspoon (5 mL) each of dried herbs

Make the dressing a day or two ahead of time to allow flavours to meld. Simply whisk all ingredients together and store, covered, in the refrigerator. Whisk again just before serving.

To assemble: Cover a large salad platter with lettuce leaves. Arrange endive leaves around edge of platter, placing a slice of mango in each leaf. Create an inner circle of avocados, placing a little dressing in each hollow. Scatter the hearts of palm and honeydew slices in between and decorate with tiger lilies or other tropical flowers.
   Pass rest of dressing separately.

Grilled Tiger Prawns

4 lbs (2.5 kg) raw tiger or extra large prawns in shells
(about 55 to 60—to serve 6 to 8)

Thread prawns on steel or wooden skewers, 4 to 5 prawns on each. If skewers are wooden, they should be well soaked in water ahead of use. Brush prawns generously with olive oil.

Oil the barbecue grill and place it 2 to 3 inches (5 to 7 cms) from the hot coals. Grill skewered prawns for 2 to 3 minutes on each side until they turn pink. Check to make sure they are cooked through: the large ones may take longer, but don't overcook. Place cooked prawns onto a platter and serve at once with slices of lemon or lime. Pass little dishes of Cantonese Dressing for dipping and supply plenty of hot baguette bread.

Note: The Grilled Vegetables (recipe on page 62) will add pizzazz to this menu. They can be cooked alongside the prawns.

Champagne Zabaglione

Quick to prepare, elegant to serve, this Italian wine custard can be served hot or cold. Marsala is the classic wine to use but Champagne makes the custard extra light, a perfect complement to fresh berries. If you serve it hot, then it's definitely a last minute proposition. Whisk it up quickly in front of your guests—everyone will enjoy the show.

Serves 6. Recipe may be doubled.

4 large egg yolks
½ cup (125 mL) champagne or sparkling wine
½ cup (125 mL) fine berry sugar

Heat a little water in a large stainless steel mixing bowl or bottom of a double boiler. Water should be very hot but not boiling. In a smaller bowl, whisk egg yolks and sugar until they are pale and foamy. Stir in the champagne and place the bowl inside the larger bowl with the hot water in it. Beat constantly with a wire whisk until the custard has doubled in bulk and begins to thicken, about 5 to 8 minutes. Remove from hot water and serve immediately, or chill to serve cold.

Fill wine goblets with fresh berries and drizzle custard over the top. I like to layer fresh raspberries or strawberries with blueberries for a colourful effect.

Après Ski

Antipasto
Lamb Shanks with Orzo
Focaccia or Italian Bread
Almond Cookie Baskets
with Italian Ice
Fresh Fruit

After a vigorous day of skiing there is nothing more gratifying than a gutsy Italian dinner. This do-ahead menu permits the chef, too, to ski all day and yet put together a dinner elegant enough for entertaining when he/she comes in. To simplify matters, visit your favourite deli for antipasto and fresh bread and prepare the main dish and dessert shells a day or so ahead of time. When it's time to eat, just pop the orzo dish into the oven and tuck into the antipasto while you wait for it to cook.

Countdown

Weeks ahead: Prepare orzo dish and freeze; make cookie baskets, pack carefully and freeze.

A day ahead: Shop for antipasto dishes from Italian deli, along with focaccia bread and Italian ice. Thaw orzo dish in refrigerator.

On day of serving: Take out cookie shells from freezer; wrap bread for heating; arrange antipasto dishes on attractive platter and garnish. Heat orzo in oven, allowing about 40 minutes. Don't spoon the ice into the cookie baskets until just before serving.

Antipasto Platter

These are some of the antipasto items I order from the deli, choosing a selection for colour, taste and texture:

Assorted olives
Sliced marinated mushrooms
Marinated calamari
Artichokes
Greek marinated dolmades
Fresh vegetables for garnish

Focaccia Bread

This Italian bread redolent with garlic and herbs is easily obtainable in city markets but here's a recipe for those who like to bake their own. Use a favourite recipe for French bread as the basis.

Ingredients to make 1 large loaf French bread
About ½ cup (125 mL) olive oil
1 tablespoon (15 mL) each of dried oregano, basil and thyme
¼ cup (60 mL) coarse sea salt
2 cloves garlic, finely chopped

Make dough for large French loaf, using olive oil instead of your usual oil or butter. When dough has risen, knead for a few minutes, then roll it out to fit a large jelly roll pan. Cover and leave to rise for 10 to 15 minutes.

Oil your fingers and poke deep holes all over the dough in rows, about an inch (2.5 cms) apart. Cover and leave to rise until doubled in bulk, about an hour.

Preheat oven to 400 degrees F. (200 degrees C.) Drizzle olive oil evenly over dough and sprinkle with salt, herbs and garlic. Bake for about 20 minutes until golden. Serve warm.

Lamb Shanks with Orzo

This dish is based on the classic Osso Buco but uses lamb shanks instead of veal and adds orzo to make a complete meal-in-one-dish. Orzo is the rice-shaped Italian pasta obtainable in most Italian specialty markets. The flavours are marvellous, and it's at its best if made a day or two ahead and reheated in the oven. Serves 8.

4 lamb shanks, each about 1 lb (500g)
¼ cup (60 mL) olive oil
4 cloves garlic, peeled and finely chopped
2 carrots, finely chopped
1 large onion, chopped (about 2 cups/500 mL)
1 28-oz (796 mL) can tomatoes, undrained, chopped
1 cup (250 mL) dry white wine
3 tablespoons (45mL) each fresh chopped oregano and thyme or 1 tablespoon (15 mL) each dried herbs
Pinch salt
Pepper to taste
2½ cups (625 mL) chicken stock
1 cup (250 mL) uncooked orzo
½ cup (125 mL) toasted pine nuts
1 cup (250 mL) freshly grated Parmesan or Asiago cheese

Remove skin and fat from lamb shanks, heat olive oil in large Dutch oven and saute shanks in olive oil until golden. Take out and set aside. Add garlic, carrots and onions to the pan and saute at low heat until soft. Put the shanks back in along with tomatoes, wine, herbs and seasonings. Cook, uncovered, in a 350 degree F. oven (180 degrees C.) for about 70 to 80 minutes.

Take out of oven, add chicken stock, orzo and bring to boil on top of the stove. Put back into the oven and continue to cook, covered, for about 25 minutes or until the orzo is soft like pasta and most of the liquid has been absorbed. There will be some liquid left but it will thicken as it cools. Cool, then refrigerate.

To serve, slice meat off the shanks and arrange on top of the orzo. Reheat in covered casserole at 350 degrees F. (180 degrees C.) for about 40 to 45 minutes or until heated through. Sprinkle top with pine nuts and pass a bowl of grated cheese. This dish freezes well. Thaw out overnight and reheat at 350 degrees F. (180 degrees C.) until heated through, about 40 minutes.

Almond Cookie Baskets

These little baskets made of crunchy almond cookies provide sweet containers for scoops of Italian ice cream, sherbert or fresh fruit. They are a bit tricky to make, but with practice they'll seem easy. Try different nuts for different flavours. The baskets can be made up to a week ahead and stored in sealed containers. They can also be frozen but stack them carefully for they are fragile.

½ cup (125 mL) butter
½ cup (125 mL) brown sugar
½ cup (125 mL) white corn syrup
7 tablespoons (105 mL) flour
1 cup (250 mL) finely chopped almonds
2 teaspoons (10 mL) vanilla

In a heavy saucepan, melt butter, add sugar and corn syrup and bring to a boil, stirring constantly. Remove from heat and add the rest of the ingredients, mixing well.

Grease and flour a large cookie sheet. Bake only two cookies at a time: they will spread out during cooking, and two are the most one can handle when it comes to shaping the baskets. For each cookie, place about 2 tablespoons (30 mL) of the batter onto the baking sheet, spreading each out into a 4-inch (10 cm) circle and pressing down with your hands to make a thin, even circle.

Bake about 10 minutes at 325 degrees F. (170 degrees C.) or until they turn golden. Watch carefully: they bake quickly. Remove from oven, place tray on wire rack to let the cookies firm up slightly for about a minute. Don't leave them longer or they will be too hard to shape.

Have ready 2 custard cups or glasses, with a bottom diameter of about 2 inches (5 cm). Slide a wide metal spatula or egg turner under one of the cookies (it should still be warm and flexible) and turn it out on top of the upside-down custard cup. With your hand, gently mold the cookie around the cup, making the bottom flat and flaring out the sides. Quickly repeat procedure with other still warm cookie. Leave cookie baskets untouched until they have hardened, then lift them gently off the cups.

Re-grease and flour the cookie sheet and continue baking cookies and forming baskets until all the batter is gone.

To serve: Fill each basket at the very last moment with a scoop of Italian ice cream or sherbet. If you fill them ahead of the time, the cookies will lose their crispness. Add a few fresh berries when in season.

Mexican Quesadillas Brunch

Mexican Beer, Sangria
Giant Quesadillas with Assorted Fillings
Avocado Salsa
Mexican Tomato Salsa
Stock Market Pesto
Applesauce
Tossed Green Salad
Fresh Fruit Platter

A big hit at Haik Gharibian's weekend brunch parties, these quesadillas can be prepared ahead of time, then dropped into the hot oil just before serving. They are a bit like deep fried, puffy sandwiches. Fillings can be sweet or savoury: use your imagination here. For condiments to go with the quesadillas, make an Avocado Salsa, pick up your favourite deli tomato salsa and basil pesto, or make the Stock Market's Hot Mexican Pesto. For the sweet tooths, make Apple Quesadillas with apple sauce, cinnamon and icing sugar. When they're ready to serve, cut them into wedges and put on a large platter. Provide Mexican beer or Sangria and a huge platter of fresh fruit. Let the party begin. Ole!

Countdown

A day ahead: Grate cheese for quesadillas; slice chicken; chop nuts.

On day of serving: Make salsa and sangria; prepare quesadillas, weight down for 30–60 minutes, then refrigerate; arrange fruit platter; fry quesadillas at the very last minute.

Sangria

This Spanish mixed drink is perennially popular, particularly on hot evenings. And it looks so nice. Serve it in a clear glass bowl. Serves 12.

1 orange
¼ cup (60 mL) white sugar
2 cups (500 mL) fresh orange juice
1 26-oz (750 mL) bottle dry red wine
½ cup (125 mL) orange flavoured liqueur
Sliced oranges, lemons and apples
Soda water

With a vegetable peeler cut off the zest of half the orange. In a bowl rub the sugar over the zest with your hands to release the oils. Add orange juice, wine and liqueur, cover and chill. Remove the orange zest after 15 minutes, then add the fruit.

Serve with a ladle, scooping up some of the fruit, and adding some ice cubes and a squirt of soda water to each glass.

Giant Mexican Quesadillas

Allow one quesadilla per person for a main entree. Cut them in wedges so that everyone can sample the different fillings. Cooking them makes quite a show. Everyone is amazed at how they puff up.

12 10-inch (25 cm) flour tortillas
3 eggs, well beaten

Filling Suggestions
green apple, sliced paper thin
Cinnamon
Finely chopped pecans, walnuts etc.

Black Forest ham, shaved (or prosciutto)
Sharp Cheddar of Mozzarella cheese, shaved
Finely chopped green onion
Salsa

Cooked chicken breasts, thinly sliced

Bottled roasted peppers, thinly sliced
Monterey Jack cheese, shaved
Salsa
Chopped canned mild green chilies

To make the quesadillas you will need pieces of wax paper and a heavy stock pot filled with water to use as a weight.

Place a sheet of wax paper on the counter and put one tortilla on top. Brush with beaten egg and add the desired filling, covering the surface to within 2 inches (5 cms) of the edge. Brush another tortilla with egg and place it over the filling. Cover with wax paper and weight down with the heavy pot. Make another five tortilla sandwiches, weighting each one down when it is finished. Leave completed quesadillas, still weighted down, for about 30 to 60 minutes.

To cook: In a very large deep Dutch oven pour two to three inches (5 to 7 cms) of light salad oil and heat until medium hot. (If the oil is too hot, the tortillas will brown too fast.) Drop the quesadillas one at a time and fry for about 1 to 2 minutes each side, using tongs to turn them over. When cooked, pat dry with paper towels, slide onto a heatproof platter and keep warm in a 300 degree F. oven (150 degrees C.) while you cook the rest.

Note: The cooked quesadillas can be reheated under the broiler for a few minutes until crisp.

Avocado Salsa

Great with the quesadillas or other Mexican foods. It must be made at the last minute or the avocados will discolour.   Makes 2 cups (500 mL).

4 large ripe avocados, peeled, seeded and mashed
1 tomato, seeded, finely chopped
4 tablespoons (60 mL) finely chopped green onion
2 large cloves of garlic, crushed
Pepper to taste
¼ teaspoon (1 mL) cumin
Pinch cayenne
2 tablespoons (30 mL) chopped cilantro
½ cup (125 mL) sour cream

Combine everything together and mix well. Serve immediately.

Stock Market's Hot Mexican Pesto

Georges and Joanne Lefebvre share with us their recipe for a different kind of pesto, one that's just great with all Mexican foods, and also for pasta dishes.

10 green jalapeno peppers, seeded
1 bunch fresh cilantro, washed
¼ cup (60 mL) cold pressed olive oil
2 tablespoons (30 mL) fresh lemon juice
2 tablespoons (30 mL) Parmesan cheese
3 tablespoons (45 mL) pumpkin seeds
Pinch of sea salt

Combine everything in a food processor and blend well. Store in the refrigerator. It will keep for several days.

Just in Case

Red Cabbage Salad with Feta Cheese
Carrot-Tomato Soup
Multi-Grain Mini Loaves
Chicken and Artichokes in Filo Paper
Fruit Chutney
Trio of Peppers Julienne
Lime Angel Pie

For emergency situations—when unexpected company arrives or we are dashing off for a weekend retreat—I rely on my freezer. Here I stash all kinds of dishes that freeze well and which can be quickly reheated. This Chicken Pie and Tomato-Carrot Soup are two of my standbys. With these on hand, all you have to do is round out the menu with a salad (this red cabbage and feta is a delight!) and your own favourite dessert and you have the makings of a delightful company occasion.

Countdown

Weeks before: Make the Tomato Soup and Chicken Pies and freeze.

Several days ahead: Make salad dressing; prepare red cabbage and store in plastic bag in refrigerator; toast pecans.

A day ahead: Bring out Chicken Pies and Soup to thaw in refrigerator. Make Angel Pie shell and Lime Filling, and refrigerate, separately.

On day of serving: In the morning, slice peppers; fill pie shell and refrigerate. An hour before serving, heat pie, and soup, warm the bread. Chop apples and cheese and finish salad; saute peppers.

Red Cabbage Salad with Feta Cheese

This unusual combination of cabbage, feta cheese and toasted pecans is combined with a tangy lemon-mustard dressing.   Serves 6 to 8.

About 4 cups (1 L) red cabbage, very thinly shredded
¾ cup (180 mL) toasted pecan halves
½ to ¾ cup (125 to 180 mL) cubed feta cheese
(if cheese is too salty, rinse well)
2 Granny Smith apples, cored and coarsely chopped (optional)

Dressing
Zest and juice of large lemon
½ cup (125 mL) peanut oil
1 tablespoon (15 mL) red wine vinegar
1 teaspoon (5 mL) Dijon mustard
2 tablespoons (30 mL) honey
pepper and pinch of salt

Combine dressing ingredients, preferably several days ahead, and store in covered jar in refrigerator. To serve: A few hours before dinner toss the cabbage with the dressing to coat well. Check seasonings. Just before serving, add cubed cheese, pecans and apples.

Carrot-Tomato Soup

This soup is thick and chunky so if you're serving it as a first course ladle out small quantities. (A big bowlful will make a meal in itself, along with bread and a tossed salad.) Make the soup in a large Dutch oven or soup pot because you'll want to prepare a large quantity—it freezes exceptionally well. But before putting it into the freezer, (I use 1- or 2-cup plastic containers) let it sit overnight in the refrigerator to allow the flavours to meld. If it seems too thick, thin it down with chicken stock.   Serves 10 to 12 for first course.

4 tablespoons (60 mL) unsalted butter *(or marg or olive oil)*
8 medium sized carrots, peeled and shredded
1 large onion, chopped
2 large leeks, white part only, cleaned and chopped
2 large cloves of garlic, peeled and chopped
Pepper and salt to taste
1 teaspoon (5 mL) ground coriander
Pinch of crushed red pepper flakes
5 medium potatoes, peeled and coarsely chopped
7 to 8 cups (1.75 to 2 L) chicken stock *(or turkey stock)*
4 large fresh tomatoes, peeled, seeded and chopped
1 28-oz (796mL) can of tomatoes, including juice

Optional:
½ teaspoon (2 mL) each of cumin and turmeric for a Middle Eastern flavour

Melt butter in a large Dutch Oven. Add carrots, onion, leeks, garlic, pepper, salt, coriander and red pepper flakes and saute for a few minutes until the onions are soft. Add potatoes and 4 cups (1L) of the chicken stock, bring to a boil, cover and cook over low heat, stirring frequently, for 10 minutes. Be careful it doesn't stick to the bottom of the pan.

Add the rest of the stock and the tomatoes. Bring back to a boil and simmer, with lid askew, for about 30 minutes or until the potatoes are cooked. Cool. Puree in small batches. Mixture should be slightly chunky. To serve, reheat until very hot, ladle into soup bowls, put a small spoonful of plain yogurt on top and swirl in with a knife. Garnish with cilantro or plain parsley. Try it with a little pesto swirled on top instead of the yogurt.

David's Chicken and Artichokes in Filo Paper

This Greek pie is my twin brother David's favourite. First served to me by my sister-in-law Dianne Matheson in Toronto, this tasty pie has been a big hit with my family ever since. And it looks as good as it tastes. I usually make two pies while I'm at it. It's no more trouble than making one, and the second pie goes into the freezer for emergencies. Fresh steamed asparagus and a tasty fruit chutney go well with this.

Serves 6 to 8.

3 whole chicken breasts
Juice and rind of 1 lemon
1 package filo pastry
3 (6½ oz, 184 mL) jars of marinated artichoke hearts *— sort - same ma, be tough.*
2 tablespoons (30 mL) chopped fresh dill or 1 teaspoon (5 mL) dried dill
½ cup (125 mL) chopped green onion

Sauce
1½ cups (375 mL) whole milk
¼ cup (60 mL) chicken stock
3 tablespoons (45 mL) butter
3 tablespoons (45 mL) flour
zest of 1 lemon
Pepper to taste

Cook chicken breasts by covering with foil and baking at 350 degrees F. (180 degrees C.) for about 40 - 45 minutes, or until tender and opaque. Don't dry out. Debone, skin and cube the meat into 1 inch (2.5 cm) chunks. Sprinkle with juice of 1 lemon and leave to cool. If you're short of time, you can buy the chicken ready cooked from the deli. Drain the artichokes and chop them into small chunks.

Make the sauce by warming the milk and stock together with the lemon zest. In a separate saucepan melt the butter and blend in the flour. Add milk mixture slowly and bring to a gentle boil, stirring constantly. When thickened, pour into a large bowl to cool. Add chicken and artichoke chunks, dill, green onions and pepper to taste.

Lightly butter both sides of 10 sheets of filo paper (I use my hands for this). As each sheet is buttered, drape one on the left hand side, another on the right hand side of a 10 inch (25 cm) springform pan, overlapping the sheets slightly in the middle. Spoon in the chicken and pat

fold in 3rds, + drape

down evenly. Bring the filo paper sheets into the middle to cover the chicken and twist them together to form a little flower. Brush with a little more butter. Bake at 375 F.(190 C) for about 40 minutes or until hot and golden.

If you plan to freeze the pie for reheating, then bake for 30 minutes or until pastry is crisp and golden then remove from oven and cool. Frozen pies should be thawed overnight in the refrigerator then reheated, covered, at 375 degrees F. (190 degrees C.) for about 30 minutes. Serve with a favourite chutney and sauteed strips of red, yellow and green bell peppers which have been lightly sauteed in a little olive oil and a pinch of red pepper flakes.

Note: To prevent the central flower from becoming too brown, cover it with foil once it has turned golden.

Lime Angel Pie

High as a cloud, this meringue pie with its tangy cream filling was one of the first pies I ever made and it's still one of my standbys. I always used to make it with lemons, but limes make a tasty change. Cook the meringue shell and the filling a day ahead but keep them separate and fill the shell just a few hours before serving. Serves 6 to 8.

Meringue
>4 large egg whites, at room temperature
>Pinch salt
>¼ teaspoon (1 mL) cream of tartar
>¾ cup (180 mL) fine berry sugar
>½ teaspoon (2 mL) vanilla

Beat egg whites until frothy, add salt and cream or tartar and continue to beat until soft peaks form. Add the sugar, a spoonful or two at a time, and beat until all the sugar is dissolved before adding the next spoonful. Continue to beat until stiff. Fold in the vanilla.

With the back of a spoon spread the meringue into a very well greased, deep, 10 inch (25 cm) glass pie plate, spreading it high on the sides in irregular peaks but not over the rim. Make a deep nest in the centre of the shell. Bake for about 60 to 70 minutes at 275 degrees F. (135 degrees C.) or until firm to the touch and sandy in colour. Turn off oven, open door slightly and leave meringue to cool. Wrap airtight and store in cupboard until ready to serve. It will keep for several days.

Filling
>6 large egg yolks
>¾ cup (180 mL) fine berry sugar
>1½ teaspoons (7 mL) lime zest, grated or chopped finely
>5 tablespoons (75 mL) lime juice
>2 cups (500 mL) whipped cream

Pour a little boiling water over the lime zest, let it sit a few minutes, then strain. This takes away the strong acid taste. In the top of a double boiler, beat the yolks and sugar until thick and lemon coloured. Add strained zest and juice and cook over hot water until thick, stirring constantly. Do not let the water touch the top saucepan. When cooked, put into a bowl, cover and refrigerate. When cold, fold in the whipped cream.

A few hours before serving, pour the lime cream custard into the meringue shell. Decorate with sliced limes, additional whipped cream and a sprinkling of shaved semi-sweet chocolate.

Something to Celebrate

Spicy Nuts
Gin-Gingered Prawns
New York Duck Salad with Crispy Wontons
Champagne or Fresh Lemon Sorbet
East meets West Rack of Lamb
or Chicken Kebobs
Peanut Satay Sauce
Oriental Fried Vegetable Brown Rice
Vicki's Creme Brulee

What an excuse we had for a special dinner party! Our son Rand's twenty-fifth birthday bash for 21 of his friends and the 25th anniversary of "The Gourmet Eight" cookbook, written by eight of us from Vancouver. These celebrations were all I needed to host two separate sit-down dinner parties in two weeks.

This East meets West menu was easy on the cook and popular with both age groups. Many of the dishes can be made in advance with just a few last minute preparations required. To simplify the work of a large sit-down affair, I highly recommend renting all the dishes, cutlery, wine glasses, linen, extra tables etc. This way there's no cleaning up to do in the wee small hours—or worse, on the morning after. It will also be a great help if you can beg, borrow or steal a couple of teenagers to help you serve. Start off the evening off with sparkling wine to set a festive mood and serve the courses leisurely.

Countdown

Weeks ahead: Make Spicy Nuts and Peanut Satay Sauce and freeze.

Days ahead: Make meat marinade and salad dressing, refrigerate; prepare salad greens and refrigerate in plastic bags.

A day ahead: Cook rice and prepare vegetables, refrigerate; make Creme Brulee, everything except the sugar topping; prepare meat for cooking; cut duck into slivers; thaw peanut satay and nuts in refrigerator.

On day of serving: In the morning, clean prawns and assemble ingredients for prawn dish, refrigerate; fry wonton skins, set aside; complete rice dish, cover and set aside; put the topping on the Creme Brulee, grill and refrigerate. In the afternoon, marinate the meat in refrigerator, turning frequently, then make chicken kebobs and refrigerate. Just before guests arrive, warm the bread, complete the preparation of prawns and hold ready to serve as appetizers (or cook the prawns right under their noses). Cook meat and keep warm; reheat rice in skillet; arrange salad.

Spicy Nuts

Nippy nibblers for holiday entertaining and as gifts, these are great to keep on hand as emergency appetizers. They can be made ahead and frozen. Makes 4 cups.

 3 tablepoons (45 mL) butter
 2 cloves garlic, crushed
 3 tablespoons (45 mL) Worcestershire sauce
 ½ teaspoon (2 mL) cinnamon
 ¼ teaspoon (1 mL) cayenne pepper
 Few drops Tabasco sauce
 4 cups (1 L) pecans, almonds or cashews, or a mixture

Preheat oven to 300 degrees F. (140 degrees C.) In a heavy skillet combine all ingredients except nuts, simmer for a few minutes, then add the nuts, tossing to coat them well. Spread on a cookie sheet and bake for 10 minutes. Turn nuts over and bake for a further 5 to 10 minutes or until slightly brown and crisp. Cool; store in airtight container or freeze.

New York Duck Salad with Crispy Wontons

The tart Lime Dressing and the barbecued duck are a perfect balance for the mixed greens and fried wontons. Barbecued duck can be purchased at most Chinese delis or meat markets, but if you can't find it, try the recipe with fresh shrimp, chicken or pork instead. It's just as good. This salad would also be excellent as a light summer main course; serve with warm baguette bread and fresh strawberry tarts for dessert.

Serves 12.

1 1lb (450 g) package Won Ton Skins
Peanut oil
1 whole barbecued duck, skinned, boned and sliced into thin strips
10 to 12 cups (2.5 to 3 L) mixed clean greens (i.e baby spinach, radicchio, leafy lettuce, butter lettuce)
½ cup (125 mL) toasted sesame seeds
¾ cup (180 mL) sliced toasted almonds
1 19 oz can (540 mL) lychee nuts, chilled and drained

Dressing
4 thin slices peeled ginger
¾ cup (180 mL) salad oil
Zest of 2 limes, chopped
½ cup (125 mL) lime juice
2 to 3 tablespoons (30 to 45 mL) honey or brown sugar
3 cloves of garlic, very finely chopped
½ teaspoon (2 mL) mild Chinese chili sauce
⅓ cup (80 mL) finely chopped shallots or green onions
¼ teaspoon (1 mL) freshly ground black pepper

The dressing should be prepared several days ahead of serving for the flavours to mellow. Soak the lime zest in boiling water for a couple of minutes, then strain. Mix all ingredients together and store in refrigerator for several days. For an unusual flavour, substitute ground Szechuan pepper for the black pepper. Remove the slices of ginger before shaking the dressing well and tossing with the greens.

The wonton skins should not be cooked until the day of serving.

First cut the skins into thin strips or wedges. Cover the base of a large skillet with about 1 inch (2.4 cm) of peanut oil and heat. (Peanut oil is best for deep frying as it does not smoke at high temperatures.)

The oil is hot enough when a strip of wonton skin begins to curl. Add strips a few at a time and deep fry only for a few seconds until they turn golden. Remove with a strainer spoon and drain well on paper towels. Put into a serving basket and set aside.

To assemble the salad: Toss greens with enough dressing to coat each leaf, then put the greens onto a large shallow platter. Cover with a layer of duck, then of almonds, then of sesame seeds and finally, with a few fried wontons. (Serve the remaining wontons in a basket.)

For a large crowd, it might be easier to divide everything up on individual salad plates.

Put the lychee nuts, impaled on toothpicks, into an attractive dish and serve as a palate refresher between the salad and the main course.

Gin-Gingered Prawns

One of my all-time hits, this appetizer or first course prawn dish hails from "down under". Prepare it at the last minute in front of your guests so the aroma of the ginger, gin and onions will titillate their taste buds. You can have everything ready to go before your guests arrive, then cook up a storm. Pickled Japanese ginger can be found at most specialty Oriental markets (or beg some from a Japanese restaurant.) Allow 5 to 6 prawns per person; about 30 medium sized prawns will serve 6.

> 4 to 5 tablespoons (60 to 75 mL) unsalted butter
> ⅔ cup (160 mL) finely chopped green onion
> 30 medium sized raw prawns, peeled
> 1 to 2 tablespoons (15 to 30 mL) pickled Japanese ginger, well drained
> 3 tablespoons (45 mL) gin
> 1 loaf baguette bread, thinly sliced and warmed

Just before serving: Melt butter in large frypan. Add onions and saute briefly. Add prawns and saute only until slightly opaque. Add ginger and gin and continue to cook for a minute or two longer, just until prawns are opaque. Do not overcook. Serve with toothpicks or in scallop shells. Pass warm bread for dipping into the sauce.

Note: For more people, if you increase the number of prawns, you must also increase the amount of sauce. There must be plenty for dipping.

Shades Of Summer, page 64. Clockwise from top: Grilled Tiger Prawns, Strawberry Zabaglione, Avocado Oriental Salad. Photographed at Haik Charibians

Apres Ski, page 67. Clockwise from top: Focaccia Bread, Lamb Shanks with Orzo, Almond Cookie Baskets, Antipasto Platter.

Mexican Quesadillas Brunch, page 71. Clockwise from top: Fruit, Avocado & Tomato Salsas, Giant Quesadillas.

Just In Case, page 75. Clockwise from top: Lime Angel Pie, Fruit Chutney, Chicken & Artichoke in Filo Paper, Trio of Peppers Julienne, Carrot Tomato Soup, Red Cabbage Salad with Feta Cheese.

Oriental Fried Vegetable Rice

On one of my visits to New York we dined at The China Grill where a cross-cultural style of cooking reigns supreme. The results are always superb. This fried rice creation, along with their Duck Salad, were voted the most popular dishes among our party that evening. This is an adaptation of the rice dish. The rice can be cooked and the vegetables chopped the day ahead. The dish can be finished on the morning of serving, kept covered in a skillet or a wok, then quickly reheated just before guests arrive. The dish goes well with any grilled meats, seafood or poultry. Serves 12. If you double it, you'll need two very large skillets.

6 cups (1.5 L) cooked brown rice*
3 tablespoons (45 mL) oil
1 cup (250 mL) carrots
1 cup (250 mL) broccoli
½ cup (125 mL) shallots
1 red pepper
1 yellow pepper
1 cup (250 mL) green onion
1 cup (150 mL) asparagus
1 teaspoon fresh ginger, finely chopped
2 cloves garlic, chopped finely
¼ teaspoon (1 mL) red pepper flakes
1 egg (optional), slightly beaten
Pinch black pepper
3 to 4 tablespoons (45 to 60 mL) Chinese light soy sauce

Cut asparagus on the diagonal into thin slices and dice the rest of the vegetables finely. They must be in very small cubes to cook quickly. Heat a large wok or skillet for 20 seconds on high heat, then add the oil. First add the diced carrots, saute for about 2 minutes, than add the rest of the vegetables, ginger, garlic and red pepper flakes and stir fry for about 2 minutes. Add beaten egg and stir. Add cooked rice and continue to stir mixture in the wok for 3 minutes. (If using a skillet, shake the pan frequently.) Add pepper and soy sauce and continue to cook for an additional 30 to 45 seconds. Transfer to heated plate and garnish as desired. Keep hot. Leftovers can be reheated, or frozen for later use.

* Note: 2½ cups (625 mL) of uncooked brown rice will yield 6 cups cooked. Rinse uncooked rice and add to 4 cups (1 L) of water. Bring to boil and simmer for 40 to 45 minutes until all liquid is absorbed.

East meets West Chicken or Lamb

The same marinade serves to flavour and tenderize chicken kebobs or rack of lamb. The same spicy Peanut Sauce goes well with either choice. Both the marinade and the sauce can be made well ahead, and both freeze well. Serves 12.

Marinade
>8 tablespoons (120 mL) light soy sauce
>14 tablespoons (210 mL) tomato sauce
>4 tablespoons (60 mL) Hoisin sauce (from Chinese markets)
>6 tablespoons (90 mL) salad or peanut oil
>3 cloves garlic, crushed

Chicken Kebobs
>6 to 8 whole chicken breasts
>(1 single chicken breast per person, plus 2 extras for second helpings)

Combine marinade ingredients. Skin and bone the chicken breasts and cut meat into cubes. Place in shallow pan and cover with the marinade. Leave for 3 to 4 hours, turning occasionally. In the afternoon of serving, thread chicken cubes onto wooden skewers and place, covered, in the refrigerator. When ready to serve, place oven on broil and grill chicken, basting from time to time and turning skewers over once. Meat should be fully cooked in about 5 to 6 minutes.

Note: Soak skewers in water for several hours to avoid burning.

Rack of Lamb
>About 5 racks of lamb
>(Allow 3 to 4 loins per person)

Put lamb racks into shallow dish and cover with marinade. Leave for 3 to 4 hours, turning occasionally. When ready to serve, set oven at 400 degrees F. (200 degrees C.) and roast meat for about 30 minutes or until meat is medium or medium rare. Don't overcook. Baste with marinade from time to time. Slice between the bones and serve.

Peanut Satay Sauce

A smooth, tasty sauce that freezes well. Whip lightly just before serving. Add extra seasonings to taste.　　　　　　　　　　　Serves 10 to 12.

1 cup (250 mL) creamy or crunchy peanut butter
1 cup (250 mL) canned coconut milk
⅓ cup (80 mL) chicken stock
3 tablespoons (45 mL) soy sauce
1 large clove garlic, minced (more to taste)
Juice of ½ lemon
Zest of 1 lemon
¼ teaspoon (1 mL) Chinese chili sauce
or ½ teaspoon (2 mL) chili powder
1 tablespoon (15 mL) brown sugar
2 teaspoons (10 mL) dark sesame oil
Black pepper to taste

Combine all ingredients in blender or food processor, reserving about a quarter of the coconut milk and stock. Blend until creamy. If sauce is too thick, dilute with some of the reserved liquids—it should be medium thick. Serve warm or at room temperature.

Vicki's Creme Brulee

It's always challenging to make food come alive on radio. When I joined the congenial Vicki Gabereau on her CBC Cross Canada afternoon show for a cooking series, her producer Rosemary Allenbach gave me the challenge. The day I walked in with Creme Brulee, Vicki's eyes lit up: I had chosen her all-time favourite dessert. Everyone listening, I'm sure, tasted every spoonful with her.

A big hit of the Fifties, this is without a doubt one of the most sensuous desserts of all time, a rich custard made with egg yolks and cream covered with a crackling lid of sweet broiled sugar. Enjoy it when you really have something to celebrate! The custard can be made the day ahead and refrigerated overnight. But don't put on the sugar topping until just before your guests arrive or it will dissolve. The sugar should be really crisp.

Serves 6 to 8.

8 egg yolks
5 tablespoons (75 mL) white sugar
3 cups (750 mL) whipping cream
1 tablespoon (15 mL) pure vanilla
About 1 cup (250mL) golden brown sugar for topping

In a double boiler or heavy saucepan combine whipping cream, sugar and vanilla and heat gently until sugar is dissolved. Keep hot, but do not boil. In a separate bowl, beat egg yolks until thick and slowly add the hot cream, stirring constantly.

Pour custard mixture into 6 to 8 small individual custard cups or ramekins and set the cups in a larger baking pan, adding boiling water to reach halfway up the sides of the cups. Bake at 325 degrees F. (160 degrees C.) for about 30 minutes or until custard is set. It should have the consistency of soft yogurt. (A knife inserted into the custard should come out clean.) Cool, then refrigerate overnight.

Several hours before serving, bring the ramekins to room temperature and press the brown sugar through a sieve onto the tops of the custards. There should be an even layer of sugar ¼ inch (6mm) thick. Broil about 4 inches (10 cm) from the heat until sugar begins to melt and the top bubbles. This will take only a minute. Watch closely to prevent burning. Chill before serving.

Note: If the sugar is sieved and placed out on a tray to dry overnight before using, the crunchy top will be that much crunchier. For variety, add a few fresh raspberries to the bottom of each custard cup before filling and baking.

Pasta, Pasta, Pasta!

Watermelon with Purple Onion
Italian Pissaladiere
Puttanesca
Valerio's Peppers with Fusilli
Spaghetti with Pommarola Sauce
Italian Bread
Baked Peaches stuffed with Amaretti Cookies
Angela Pia

"Saturday Night Specials" from my kitchen often include Italian Pissaladiere, a cross between a tart and a pizza, and then one of the robust pasta dishes for which Italy is famous. Choose Puttanesca, Peppers with Fusilli or Spaghetti with Pommarola, the classic tomato sauce. With plenty of Italian bread and wine and perhaps a light fruit mousse dessert, this menu will stir up memories of intimate dinners at small family restaurants tucked away in the villages of the Chianti vineyard country.

Countdown

Weeks ahead: Make the tomato-onion base for the Pissaladiere and freeze; make the Pommarola Sauce and freeze.

A day ahead: Grate the fresh Parmesan, refrigerate; make Angela Pia; crush the Amaretti cookies; thaw Pommarola in refrigerator.

On day of serving: In the morning, make Puttanesca, if serving, and refrigerate; if serving the Peppers with Fusilli, prepare the peppers. Assemble Pissaladieres and refrigerate; prepare watermelon platter, cover and keep at room temperature; wrap bread for oven heating. Before guests arrive, prepare peaches, sprinkle with lemon juice, cover and refrigerate. The final preparation and cooking of the pasta dishes and the baked peaches can be done at the last moment.

Watermelon with Purple Onions

An unusual and very refreshing combination of flavours. Throughout the south of Italy, roadside watermelon stands are part of the landscape. You sit down beside a long, smooth table and the owner chops off slices of watermelon and slides them down the table for you to catch and eat. The stands are always packed with people in the summer, not only eating the sweet, cool melon but catching up on the latest soccer game tactics.

Our presentation is a bit more sophisticated than this, but watermelon is still fun to eat. Scoop out the watermelon into small balls and pile them into a mound on a large serving platter. Sprinkle with very thinly sliced purple onion rings and decorate the platter with Italian parsley.

Italian Pissaladiere

I've borrowed from the traditional French cuisine and added a touch of Italian to the traditional Provencal tart. The Pissaladiere is a cross between a tart and a pizza and it is always a big hit. It is perfect as an appetizer or with soup and salad for a complete meal. The tomato-onion base can be frozen to keep on hand for emergencies. It also makes a great condiment to serve with barbecued salmon or roast meats. As well, stock your freezer with ready made pizza crusts and focaccia bread.

Ready made pizza crusts

Base

3 tablespoons (45 mL) olive oil
6 large white onions, thinly sliced
1 tablespoon (15 mL) sugar
4 or more large cloves of garlic, chopped finely
1 14-oz (392 mL) tin plum tomatoes, chopped, undrained
2 tablespoons (30 mL) tomato paste
1/8 teaspoon (.5 mL) crushed red pepper flakes
1 teaspoon (5 mL) sugar
1 teaspoon each (5 mL) of dried basil, thyme, oregano or 1 tablespoon (15 mL) each fresh herbs
Salt and pepper to taste

In a large skillet, heat oil, add onions, sugar and garlic and mix well. Cover and simmer over low heat for about 25 to 30 minutes until onions are soft and golden. Stir frequently.

In a small saucepan, combine tinned tomatoes with the rest of the ingredients and simmer for 10 to 15 minutes or until reduced in volume to about 1 cup (250 mL). Add tomato mixture to the onions, mix well and simmer for a few minutes to blend. This will make about 3 cups (750 mL). Refrigerate or freeze in 1 cup (250 ml) containers.

To make the pissaladiere: Spread a layer of the tomato-onion mixture onto a pizza crust or focaccia bread, add extra toppings and heat at 400 degrees F. (200 degrees C.) for about 8 to 10 minutes to heat through. Slice into small wedges and serve hot.

Suggested Toppings
1: *Canned anchovies, drained and chopped black olives*
2: *Sun-dried tomatoes, chopped, small slivers of goat cheese and fresh basil.*
3: *Grated Parmesan or Asiago cheese, slices of chopped prosciutto and toasted pinenuts*
4: *Chopped fresh tomatoes, fresh basil, mozzarella cheese, Parmesan or Asiago cheese and a sprinkling of pesto.*

Puttanesca
(Pasta of the Night)

The story goes that the women of the night in Siena, Italy, wanted a dish that was cheap, quick to prepare, high in calories for quick energy and tasted scrumptious. They came up with this recipe. Taste it, and judge for yourself. Serves 6 to 8.

> 8 to 10 medium sized tomatoes or 14 roma tomatoes, sliced about ⅓ inch (8 mm) thick
> 2 cans anchovies, drained, patted dry and chopped
> ½ cup (125 mL) or more black olives, halved
> 4 or more large cloves of garlic, finely chopped
> ¼ to ½ teaspoon (1 to 2 mL) crushed red pepper flakes
> Fresh or dried basil, lots
> Black pepper to taste
> Olive oil
> 1½ lbs (750 g) dried spaghetti or fettucine
> ¾ to 1 cup (180 to 250 mL) Parmesan or Asiago cheese

Set oven to 350 degrees F. (180 degrees C.) In a large lasagne-type pan make two layers of all the ingredients except for the pasta and the cheese, beginning with the tomatoes and ending with the basil. Drizzle both layers well with olive oil and sprinkle with pepper. Bake for about 30 to 35 minutes while you cook the spaghetti or fettucine. Drain cooked pasta, place on a large serving platter and toss with a little olive oil and some of the cheese. Chop up the cooked tomato mixture well and add to the pasta along with about 4 to 6 more tablespoons (60 to 90 mL) of cheese. Add more chopped fresh basil to taste. There will be lots of tomato juices. Serve with heated Italian bread to mop up the juices and pass more cheese.

This dish is excellent for carbohydrate loading before a big race.

If you are in a super hurry, as the Siena girls may have been from time to time, simply chop all the sauce ingredients and throw into a heavy skillet. Simmer for ten minutes or so until thickened and while the spaghetti cooks.

Note: Do not leave out the anchovies. Their strong flavour disappears in the cooking — even anchovy haters won't be able to taste them. But they add a zesty touch. The dish won't be the same without them.

Valerio's Peppers with Fusilli

During our visit to Auckland, New Zealand for the Commonwealth Games, the distance runners and their coaches celebrated their victory at Valerio's, a well-known Italian restaurant in the Parnell district. Valerio's "Italian" chefs, one from Morocco, one from China, created some outstanding dishes for our athletes. This was one we particularly liked. And it's quick and easy. Serves 4 hungry athletes.

1lb (600 g) dried fusilli (spiral noodles), cooked according to directions
5 tablespoons (75 mL) olive oil
4 cloves garlic, finely chopped
1 large onion, chopped
¼ teaspoon (1 mL) crushed red pepper flakes
3 small green chili peppers, (jalapeno or serrano)
  seeded, chopped finely
4 red peppers, sliced julienne style or 2 red peppers, 2 yellow peppers
¾ cup (180 mL) dry white wine
¾ cup (180 mL) basic tomato sauce (recipe follows)
Salt and pepper to taste
Freshly grated Parmesan or Asiago cheese

In a large skillet, heat the olive oil. Add garlic, onion and chili peppers and saute for a few minutes. Add the peppers and saute for a few minutes longer. Add wine, tomato sauce, salt and pepper and simmer for about another 10 minutes. Toss with the pasta and sprinkle with Parmesan cheese.

Pommarolo
(Basic Tomato Sauce)

This is the basic tomato sauce that I freeze as a base for pizza, pasta sauces etc. It's spicy, tangy and fresh.   Makes about 6 cups (1.5 L.)

3 tablespoons (45 mL) olive oil
1 medium onion, chopped
4 large cloves garlic, finely chopped
2 green jalapeno or serrano peppers, seeded and chopped
3 tablespoons (45 mL) each fresh basil and oregano
   or 1½ teaspoons (7 mL) each of dried herbs
1/8 teaspoon (.5 mL) crushed red pepper flakes
1 teaspoon (5 mL) sugar
10 large tomatoes, peeled, seeded and coarsely chopped
1 14-oz (398 mL) can Italian tomatoes, chopped, undrained
½ cup (125 mL) dry red or white wine

Heat oil in large skillet. Add onions, garlic, peppers, herbs, pepper flakes and sugar and saute over low heat until vegetables are softened, about 10 minutes. Add fresh and canned tomatoes and wine and simmer, uncovered, for about 30 minutes. Puree in food processor just until slightly chunky. Freeze in 1 cup (250 mL) containers.

Note: for easy peeling and seeding of tomatoes, follow this procedure: Slash the bottoms of each tomato with an x and cut out the core. Put tomatoes into a large bowl or pan and cover with boiling water. Leave for about 30 seconds or until the skins start to peel away. Drain water and peel off skin. Cut tomatoes in half horizontally and squeeze out the seeds. Chop coarsely.

Chicken Vegetable Saute

To add variation to your basic pasta with tomato sauce, try this quick topping. You'll need 1 lb (500 g) pasta and 1½ to 2 cups (375 to 500 mL) tomato sauce to serve 4 people. While the sauce is heating and the pasta cooking, throw the following into a skillet along with 2 tablespoons (30 mL) of olive oil: 1 cup (250 mL) chicken breasts, boned, skinned and sliced julienne. Saute until meat is opaque, then add 1 red or yellow pepper, sliced julienne, 6 to 8 large mushrooms, quartered, ½ cup (125 mL) of fresh basil (or 1 tablespoon (15 mL) dried basil) and 2 large cloves of garlic, finely chopped. Saute for 2 to 3 minutes. Add the juice of 1 lemon and ¼ cup (60 mL) Marsala. Simmer for a few minutes more, then keep warm.

Mix the cooked, drained pasta with the hot tomato sauce and put onto a large dish. Top with the chicken saute, sprinkle with Parmesan cheese and serve.

Baked Peaches stuffed with Amaretti Cookies

A quick dessert with a distinctly Italian taste. Serves 6.

6 whole fresh ripe peaches
4 to 5 tablespoons (60 to 75 mL) lemon juice
1½ cups (375 mL) Amaretti cookies
2 tablespoons (30 mL) brown sugar
⅓ cup (80 mL) softened butter
Amaretto liqueur

Early in the day, peel, seed and halve the peaches and dip in lemon juice. Put into a shallow casserole. Combine cookies, sugar and butter and blend well. Fill the hollow of each peach half with about 1 tablespoon (15 mL) of the filling and sprinkle a little liqueur over each. Bake, uncovered, for about 30 minutes at 375 degrees F. (190 degrees C.) or until peaches are softened and golden. Serve with Italian peach ice cream or Angela Pia.

Angela Pia

When Doug interned in San Francisco many years ago, we went often to Pietro's restaurant, famous for its Italian cuisine. We invariably ended the evening with Pietro's classic Angela Pia dessert, which is wickedly delicious, a bit like Syllabub or Zabaglione.   Serves 6.

3 eggs, separated
½ cup (125 mL) white sugar
2 tablespoons (30 mL) brandy
2 tablespoons (30 mL) white rum
1 tablespoon (15 mL) unflavoured gelatine
¼ cup (60 mL) cold water
1 cup (250 mL) whipping cream
1 teaspoon (15 mL) vanilla

Beat egg yolks until light and lemon coloured, add sugar gradually and continue to beat until thick and creamy. Add brandy and rum. In a small saucepan soak the gelatine in the cold water and stir over low heat until gelatine is dissolved. Cool slightly, then add to the egg mixture.

Beat whipping cream with the vanilla until thick, then fold into the egg mixture. Beat egg whites until stiff, then fold in the egg yolk mixture gently but thoroughly. Pour into wine goblets and chill for several hours or overnight. It's good alone but it's wonderful with a few fresh strawberries or raspberries.

Orient Expression

Chilled Champagne Melon Soup
Sesame Rice Crackers
Asian Salad with Grilled Chicken Strips
Baguette Bread
Ju Ju Chocolate Sushi

From the Cin Cin restaurant (Cheers, Cheers) in Auckland, New Zealand and the Ju Ju Cafe (Sizzle Sizzle) in Vancouver, comes the inspiration for this summertime Oriental menu. For starters, the Champagne Melon soup is light and refreshing. The Asian Salad, my version of the Cin Cin's, is a meal all by itself, with lots of crunchy vegetables and grilled chicken strips tossed in a ginger-curry dressing. The unique Chocolate Sushi from the Ju Ju Cafe looks exquisite and tastes heavenly, a real joy for lovers of marzipan.

Countdown

Several days ahead: Make Chocolate Sushi and Salad Dressing; toast nuts and sesame seeds and clean salad greens, storing in the refrigerator.

A day ahead: Prepare the rest of the vegetables for the salad.

On day of serving: In the morning, make soup; prepare chicken breasts and marinate. Just before guests arrive, warm the bread; grill chicken and cut into strips just before adding to tossed salad. Break salad greens into bite-sized pieces.

Chilled Champagne Melon Soup

A quick summer soup to make when strawberries are at their sweetest. Serves 6 to 8.

2 to 3 cantaloupes, peeled and cubed (about 6 cups/1.5 L)
2 cups (500 mL) fresh strawberries
⅓ cup (80 mL) buttermilk
⅓ cup (80 mL) champagne or sparkling white wine
Fresh mint for garnish

Several hours before serving, puree the fruit. Gradually add enough of the buttermilk and champagne to give a thick soup-like consistency. Refrigerate. Serve in melon halves or small bowls garnished with a sprig of fresh mint.

Asian Salad with Grilled Chicken Strips

There we were, sitting at the popular Cin Cin restaurant on Auckland's waterfront, enjoying the chef's special salad and watching the sailing ships pass by. It was a perfect summer evening. We sipped our New Zealand chardonnay and lingered over the sunset. We liked the salad so much I brought the recipe idea home with me. My version is a meal in itself, served with strips of freshly-grilled chicken. Serves 6 to 8.

Dressing
1 cup (250 mL) mayonnaise (must be the real stuff)
½ to ¾ cup (125 to 180 mL) plain yogurt
½ cup (125 mL) salad oil
2 to 3 tablespoons (30 to 45 mL) coconut milk or plain milk
⅓ cup (80 mL) chicken stock
2 tablespoons (30 mL) fresh lime juice
Zest of 1 lime
2 teaspoons (10 mL) curry powder, or to taste
1 tablespoon (15 mL) honey
1 teaspoon (5 mL) grated fresh ginger
2 teaspoons (10 mL) mild Chinese chili sauce
Pepper to taste
1 tablespoon (15 mL) sesame oil

One or two days ahead of serving, soak lime zest in boiling water for a few minutes; drain and chop. Mix all ingredients together, whisking until well blended. Refrigerate.

Salad Ingredients
    2 heads romaine lettuce, cleaned and dried
    1 radicchio, cleaned and dried
    2 Belgian endives, cut into julienne strips
    1½ cups (375 mL) Chinese dried crispy noodles
    ½ cup (125 mL) toasted cashews or almonds
    4 tablespoons (60 mL) toasted sesame seeds
    1½ cups fresh asparagus, chopped on the diagonal and blanched
    1 small zucchini, cut into small slivers
    4 single chicken breasts, boned and skinned
    1 tablespoon (15 mL) light soy sauce
    1 tablespoon (15 mL) sesame oil
    Garnish: red peppers, cut julienne and sesame seeds

On the day of serving, marinate the chicken breasts in the soy sauce and sesame oil for an hour or two. Grill or saute until cooked, then cut into thin strips. Set aside. Assemble salad ingredients in a large bowl ready to toss at the last moment with just enough salad dressing to coast. Top salad with chicken strips, sprinkle with an additional 2 tablespoons (30 mL) toasted sesame seeds and decorate with sliced peppers for additional colour.
    Serve with fresh baguette bread or puffed shrimp crackers (obtainable from Oriental markets).

Note: For salad variations you can throw in many different extras, such as slivers of red and yellow peppers, baby Chinese corn or bean sprouts.

Ju Ju Chocolate Sushi

One of the most popular East meets West restaurants in Vancouver is the Ju Ju Cafe. My favourite luncheon dish there is a wonderful crepe topped with grilled vegetables, seafood or meat with a special sauce. And I always succumb to the temptation of their Chocolate Sushi for dessert. The recipe was given to me by chefs Georges Bourque and Dennis Bond, and I herewith pass it along. They present the sushi on a small rectangular plate, along with swirls of bitter chocolate. The two-layer chocolate and marzipan rolls filled with glazed fruit and coated with chocolate can be made in advance and stored in the refrigerator; slice and decorate just before the guests arrive.

Layer One
> 12 oz (350 g) marzipan or almond paste, at room temperature
> 4 oz (115g) unsweetened long shredded coconut
> 2 tablespoons (30 mL) sugar syrup (available in gourmet food sections, or use white corn syrup)

Knead well until smooth. Set aside.

Layer Two
> 3 oz (85 g) semi-sweet chocolate, melted
> 6 oz (170 g) marzipan or almond paste, at room temperature.

Mix together and knead well. Set aside.

Filling
> Candied angelica
> Candied red cherries

(The idea is to imitate the fillings in real sushi)

Coating
> Semi-sweet chocolate, melted
> Shredded coconut
> Sesame seeds

Spread counter with two layers of plastic wrap. Roll out Layer One to a sheet 8 by 4 inches (20 by 10 cms); it will be ¼ inch (6 mm) thick. Roll out Layer Two to same dimension, but it will be only half as thick.

Stack Layer One on top of Layer Two, offsetting them so that 1 inch (2.5 cms) of the narrow end of the top layer projects. With this edge towards you, place the cherry and angelica filling in place, fold over projecting lip of top layer, then roll both layers up together like a jelly roll, using the plastic wrap to help you achieve a close, smooth roll.

Quickly roll the sushi in melted chocolate to coat and cut roll into two pieces. Roll one in coconut, the other in sesame seeds. When chocolate is set, wrap well and refrigerate.

To serve: Drizzle melted chocolate into a free-form design on an oblong Oriental plate and leave until chocolate has set. Cut rolls into ½ inch (12 mm) slices like sushi and arrange on prepared plate. Decorate with whole strawberries, star fruit or other fruit. Provide small dishes of warm melted chocolate for dipping.

Cross-Culture Cuisine

Fresh Asparagus with Peanut Dressing
Rice Crackers
Spicy Noodles with Prawns and Pork
Multigrain Bread
Strawberry Rhubarb Tart

This zesty noodle dish offers an interesting Oriental change of pace from the classic Italian pasta and sauce. Soy, chili sauce and ginger add spice to Italian linguine noodles, with prawns and pork strips for protein and flavour. To complete the cross-cultural theme, serve fresh asparagus with a spicy peanut dressing. The dessert: a scrumptious French strawberry rhubarb tart, a classic that never fades.

Everything on this menu can be made in advance: all that is left for the last minute is to assemble the noodle dish and steam the asparagus.

Countdown

Several days ahead: Make Peanut Dressing, pie crust and Rhubarb filling and store in refrigerator.

A day ahead: Make sauce for noodles and Vanilla Custard and refrigerate.

On day of serving: In the morning, prepare asparagus; prepare prawns and pork and steep in marinade. Complete pie.

Asparagus with Peanut Dressing

This appetizer rates a 10 in our house. Make the dressing a day or two ahead of time, lightly steam the asparagus and let guests dip into the dressing themselves. For a sensational serving idea serve the asparagus standing up in a small hollowed out pumpkin, with the dressing on the side. Note: it is perfectly polite on informal occasions to pick the asparagus up with your fingers. Serves 6 to 8.

Dressing
½ cup (125 mL) chunky peanut butter
1 tablespoon (15 mL) soy sauce
1 tablespoon (15 mL) sesame oil
1 teaspoon (5 mL) lemon juice
2 cloves garlic, crushed
1 teaspoon (5 mL) Chinese chili sauce
2 tablespoons (30 mL) brown sugar
1 cup (250 mL) plain yogurt
2 tablespoons (30 mL) toasted sesame seeds

Combine all ingredients in a food processor or blender, cover and store in the refrigerator. To serve, bring to room temperature and thin out with a little yogurt if necessary.

36–42 asparagus spears (allow 6 per person)
Zest of 1 lemon
½ cup (125 mL) toasted sesame seeds
1 leafy or butter lettuce

On the day of serving, trim and clean the asparagus and simmer for a minute or two in boiling water until just tender-crisp. Don't overcook. Drain and chill in ice water. Pat dry and refrigerate. Serve the asparagus on a large lettuce lined platter, with the dressing in a bowl in the centre. Sprinkle sesame seeds and lemon zest over the asparagus. Let everyone help themselves, using their fingers to dip the asparagus into the sauce.

For more formal occasions, divide the asparagus between 6 small salad plates, garnish with lettuce and drizzle with the sauce, sesame seeds and lemon zest.

Rand's Spicy Noodles with Prawns and Pork

This dish ranked in the Top Five of my family's choice of recipes from this book. It makes a satisfying meal all by itself but it's also good served with steamed fresh asparagus or snow peas. Chicken can be substituted for either the prawns or the pork. Serves 6 to 8.

25 to 30 raw prawns, peeled
1 tablespoon (15 mL) Chinese rice wine vinegar
3 thin slices ginger, chopped finely
About 1 lb (500 g) pork tenderloin (or 2 small whole chicken breasts, boned and skinned)
2 teaspoons (10 mL) dry sherry
1½ teaspoons (7 mL) cornstarch
1 teaspoon (5 mL) sesame oil

Marinate prawns in vinegar and ginger. Cut pork tenderloin into thin strips and marinate in sherry, cornstarch and oil. Cover dishes, refrigerate and leave for 30 minutes to an hour.

Sauce

2 cups (500 mL) chicken stock
3 tablespoons (45 mL) soy sauce
1 tablespoon (15 mL) tomato paste
½ tablespoon (7mL) sugar
2 teaspoons (10 mL) mild Chinese chili sauce
1 tablespoon (15 mL) sesame oil
3 tablespoons (45 mL) cornstarch
3 tablespoons (45 mL) cold water

Combine all ingredients except cornstarch and water in a small heavy saucepan and stir over medium heat until hot. Blend cornstarch with water and add to the sauce, stirring well and cooking until sauce is thick and clear. This sauce can be made ahead and refrigerated. Reheat to serve.

Vegetable Mixture
   1 tablespoon (15 mL) sesame oil
   4 tablespoons (60 mL) peanut oil or safflower oil
   2 cloves garlic, finely chopped
   2 teaspoon (10 mL) fresh ginger, finely chopped
   ¼ teaspoon (1mL) crushed dried red pepper flakes
   ½ cup (125 mL) white onion, thinly sliced
   1 small leek, cut into julienne strips (about 1 cup/250 mL)
   ½ red pepper, in julienne strips
   ½ yellow pepper, in julienne strips

Garnish
   Toasted sesame seeds
   ½ cup (125 mL) green onions, sliced on the diagonal

To assemble: Cook 1½ lbs (750 g) egg linguine or fettucine according to directions. This can be done early on the day of serving. When cooked, rinse with cold water and toss with 1 tablespoon (15 mL) of sesame oil. (If cooking at the last minute, omit the cold rinse.)

Remove prawns and pork from marinate and drain well. In large skillet, heat sesame and peanut oils and saute the prawns until opaque. Set aside. Saute the pork tenderloin strips in same pan, adding more peanut oil if needed. Set aside. Add the vegetables to the pan and stir fry until the onions are softened. Add the sauce to the skillet along with the cooked pork and prawns. Toss in the cooked noodles and stir well over medium heat until hot throughout. Toss well to blend the sauce with the noodles.

To serve: pour onto a large pasta plate and sprinkle with sesame seeds and green onions.

Strawberry Rhubarb Tart

When local strawberries and rhubarb are at their peak of sweetness, treat your family to this classic delight. The shell, rhubarb filling and the custard can be made ahead and chilled separately. Fill the pie and glaze the fruit on the day of serving. Serves 6 to 8.

Pie Shell
½ cup (125 mL) soft butter
3 tablespoons (45 mL) dark brown sugar
½ cup (125 mL) finely chopped toasted almonds or hazelnuts
1 large egg, beaten
¼ teaspoon (1 mL) almond extract
1⅓ cups (325 mL) all purpose flour

Butter a 10-inch (25 cm) quiche or tart pan with a removable bottom. In a mixing bowl or food processor cream butter and sugar, add nuts, egg and extract. Mix in flour and blend well. Press dough into the pan, distributing it evenly over the bottom and up the sides about 2 inches (5 cm). Chill for 30 minutes, then bake at 375 degrees F. (180 degrees C.) for about 15 to 20 minutes or until golden. Cool.

Custard Filling
2 large egg yolks
3 tablespoons (45 mL) white sugar
2½ tablespoons (37 mL) cornstarch
1 teaspoon (5 mL) vanilla
⅔ cup (160 mL) milk, heated
4 tablespoons (60 mL) unsalted butter, at room temperature

Beat the first four ingredients in a medium saucepan until pale yellow in colour. Add warm milk gradually, mixing well to blend. Stir over medium heat until thickened, and smooth, about 6 to 8 minutes. Add butter, a tablespoon (15 mL) at a time, beating well with a wire whisk. Pour into a bowl, leave to cool, then cover and refrigerate.

Rhubarb Filling
4 cups (1 L) fresh rhubarb, cut into ½ inch (12 mm) pieces
¾ cup (180 mL) white sugar
Pinch salt
1 tablespoon plus 1 teaspoon (20 mL) cornstarch
¼ cup (60 mL) water

In a saucepan combine rhubarb, sugar and salt. Leave to stand for a few minutes to release some juice. Combine cornstarch with the water and add to rhubarb. Bring to boil over medium heat, stirring constantly. Reduce heat to low, cover and simmer, stirring frequently, until rhubarb is tender and liquid thickened, about 10 minutes. Cool, then refrigerate.

Topping
4 cups (1 L) strawberries
1 cup (250 mL) red currant jelly, melted and cooled

To assemble: Release crust from pie pan. Pour in the cold custard filling, spreading evenly. Cover with the rhubarb filling and arrange the berries carefully on top, making concentric circles to cover. Chill. Using a pastry brush, lightly glaze the berries with the cool currant jelly, coating the entire top surface of the pie. (If the jelly is too hot, it will disturb the fillings.) Chill pie until ready to serve.

Drop over for Brunch!

When does breakfast end and brunch begin? Before 11 am is breakfast and from 11 to 2 pm is brunch, but it doesn't really matter what you call it. For sure, it's fast becoming a very popular occasion for entertaining friends and family, particularly on leisurely Sundays.

It may be after a vigorous morning of exercise, or just lazing around, catching up on the newspapers. It's a time to put your feet up and relax, so let everyone pitch in and help with the cooking, setting the table or squeezing the orange juice.

Plan the meal around one easy central dish and include plenty of fresh fruit, assorted breads, homemade jams, freshly-ground coffee or, for special occasions, champagne and orange juice.

Better have a big pot of soup on hand though, because everyone may be having such a good time they might just decide to stay on for dinner!

Here are some of my favourite breakfast and brunch dishes.

Classic French Toast for Four

In a large shallow bowl whisk about ⅔ cup (160 mL) of milk with 5 beaten eggs. Add 1 teaspoon (5 mL) vanilla, ¼ teaspoon (1 mL) cinnamon, a pinch of nutmeg and 3 to 4 teaspoons (15 to 20 mL) sugar. Cut day-old bread into thick slices and put into the egg mixture, soaking each piece well. Let sit for 30 minutes, covered.

Melt about 3 to 4 tablespoons (45 to 60 mL) of unsalted butter in a skillet and saute the soaked bread over medium heat until golden, then flip over and cook the other side. Serve immedietely, or if you are doing a large batch, cover the toast with foil and keep warm in a low oven.

To serve, sprinkle with icing sugar and offer a variety of jam, maple or fruit syrups, even whipped cream for a treat.

Be sure to cut the bread about ½ inch (12 mm) thick so it will absorb the egg mixture. For really light toast, let the bread soak for about half an hour in the egg batter.

Instead of regular white bread, try raisin-cinnamon bread or use croissants, cut in half.

Dad's Famous Family French Toast

Dad is 83, looks 63, and enjoys life to the fullest. He walks five miles several days a week, follows a good healthy diet and is still an avid writer for numerous periodicals. Pati, our stepmother and Dad enjoy making the family breakfast whenever we visit them in Montreal. While Pati organizes the rest of the treats for us, Dad whips up his family's favourite French Toast. It's a real winner. This is his (previously) secret recipe. It serves 4.

Whites of 6 eggs
Yokes of 4 eggs
Dash of cinnamon
Dash of nutmeg
6 slices of French bread or home-made bread, ½ inch (12 mm) thick
¾ cup (180 mL) low fat milk
4 tablespoons (60 mL) Parmesan cheese
1 tablespoon (15 mL) or less of butter
1 cup (250 mL) fresh or thawed frozen strawberries
Scoops of vanilla ice cream or yogurt

Whip the egg whites until stiff. Set aside. Mix the egg yolks with spices, milk and cheese then fold into the egg whites, blending carefully. Pour the egg mixture over the bread and leave until thoroughly soaked.

Heat an electric skillet to 400 degrees F. (200 degrees C.), or use a heavy frypan, and add enough butter to lightly coat the bottom. Pan should be hot enough to seize each side of the soaked bread. Saute bread quickly on both sides and serve hot, topped with a scoop of ice cream or yogurt and some strawberries.

California Sandwich Bake

Always popular with athletes, this cheese and egg combination can be prepared the evening before and baked just before serving. Chopped ham or chicken make interesting additions. Serves 6 to 8.

About 1lb (500 g) Monterey Jack cheese, thinly sliced 2 4-oz (125g) cans mild green chili peppers, chopped and drained
4 large eggs
2 cups (500 mL) milk
1 teaspoon (5 mL) Dijon mustard
Pinch salt
Pinch pepper
12 ½-inch (12 mm) slices of French bread

On the day ahead, arrange six slices of bread on the bottom of a well-greased lasagne-size pan. Add a layer of half the cheese slices and sprinkle peppers over the cheese. Cover with remaining bread slices. Beat eggs with milk, mustard, salt and pepper and pour over the bread and cheese mixture. Cover pan and let sit in the refrigerator for up to 24 hours.

Bake in a 350 degree F. (180 degree C.) oven for about 25 to 30 minutes or until it is puffed and set. Serve immediately and pass the Mexican salsa.

Sauteed sweet peppers go well with this.

Ruth Matheson's Morning Glory Muffins

Moist and full of flavour, these muffins are meals in themselves, perfect for that mid-morning snack. Makes about 24.

4 cups (1L) flour
2½ cups (625 mL) sugar
4 teaspoons (60 mL) baking soda
4 teaspoons (60 mL) cinnamon
¼ teaspoon (5 ml) salt
4 grated carrots
1 cup (250 mL) raisins
1 cup (250 mL) chopped pecans
1 cup (250 mL) coconut
2 apples, peeled, cored and grated
6 large eggs
2 cups (500 mL) vegetable oil
4 teaspoons (60 mL) vanilla

Sift the dry ingredients and stir in the carrots, raisins, pecans, coconut and grated apples. Beat eggs with oil and vanilla and stir into the flour mixture. Spoon into muffin pans and bake at 350 degrees F. (180 degrees C.) for 35 minutes. Let cool for 5 minutes in the pans, then turn out onto wire racks. These freeze very well.

Cranberry Loaf

This tart cranberry loaf manages to satisfy most sweet cravings and is ideal for breakfasts and brunches, as well as lunch packs. It keeps moist for days and freezes well. Try it toasted.   Makes 1 loaf.

2 cups (500 mL) all purpose flour
¾ cup (180 mL) brown sugar
2 teaspoons (10 mL) baking powder
1 teaspoon (5 mL) baking soda
¼ teaspoon (1 mL) salt
¼ teaspoon (1 mL) cinnamon
¼ teaspoon (1 mL) nutmeg
1 large egg, beaten
¾ cup (180 mL) buttermilk
3 tablespoons (45 mL) corn oil or melted butter
1 cup (250 mL) coarsely-chopped cranberries, fresh or frozen

Blend dry ingredients in large bowl. Mix together the egg, milk and oil and stir into the dry ingredients, mixing just enough to blend. Lightly fold in the cranberries.

Turn into a greased loaf pan and bake at 350 degrees F. (180 degrees C.) for about 50 minutes or until it tests done with a straw. Cool. Wrap well in foil.

Ruth's Granola

Although granola can be high in sugar and fat, it is also high in nutrients and fibre from whole grains, fruits and nuts. Sprinkle a little on some yogurt and top with a sprinkle of cinnamon to satisfy your sweet tooth. This is a Matheson breakfast treat, from Halifax to Vancouver

6 cups (1.5 L) oats, large flake or regular
1 cup (250 mL) wheatgerm
1 cup (250 mL) nuts (almonds, walnuts, pecans etc.)
1 cup (250 mL) unsalted sunflower seeds
1 cup (250 mL) unsweetened coconut
¾ cup (180 mL) safflower oil
¼ cup (60 mL) brown sugar
¼ cup (60 mL) honey
1 teaspoon (5 mL) vanilla
1 cup (250 mL) raisins

Mix all dry ingredients together in a large roasting pan. Mix oil, honey and vanilla and pour over the top, mixing well with the hands to coat. Bake at 275 degrees F. (135 degrees C.) for 30 minutes, turning every ten minutes. Cool and store in sealed containers.

Gold Medal Buttermilk Pancakes

What would breakfast be without pancakes? Athletes devour these for carbo-loading when training or after a long run. Watch them disappear. Makes about 18 4-inch (10 cm) pancakes.

2 cups (500 mL) all-purpose flour
1 teaspoon (5 mL) baking soda
Pinch of salt
2 tablespoons (30 mL) white sugar
2 large eggs, slightly beaten
2 cups (500 mL) buttermilk
2 tablespoons (30 mL) melted butter

Combine dry ingredients in a bowl. Add eggs, buttermilk and melted butter and stir only until flour is barely moistened. Never mind a few lumps. Let mixture sit for at least 10 minutes.

Bake on a hot, lightly greased griddle. Preferably the griddle or pan should be heavy cast iron and hot enough so that a drop of water skitters on the surface. If you're using an electric frypan, set the temperature to 375 degrees F. (190 degrees C.)

For uniform pancakes, use a ¼ cup (60 mL) measure. Flip over the pancakes when the bubbles burst on the surface, about a minute, and cook until golden brown on both sides, about 2 minutes total.

For variety, add 1 cup (250 mL) of fresh blueberries to the batter.

Serve with lots of pure maple syrup or special trimmings.

Trimmings for Pancakes and French Toast

Maple Syrup with Toasted Almonds
2 cups (500 mL) pure maple syrup
½ cup (125 mL) sliced almonds, toasted
2 cinnamon sticks

While pancakes are cooking, put syrup, almonds and cinnamon sticks into a small saucepan and heat gently for 5 to 10 minutes to blend the flavours.

Sauteed Bananas
In a skillet, melt 3 tablespoons (45 mL) of butter, add 3 bananas, peeled and sliced lengthwise, then cut in half. Saute for a few minutes, then add 2 to 3 tablespoons (30 to 45 mL) of brown sugar and a dash of white rum, orange liqueur, or orange juice. Simmer for a minute or two to caramelize. Serve with pancakes or French toast. Enough for 3 to 4 servings.

Fried Apples
In a skillet, melt 3 tablespoons (45 mL) of butter. Add 4 Granny Smith or Newton apples, cored and cut into eighths (no need to peel) and saute for about 5 minutes. Sprinkle over 2 tablespoons (30 mL) of brown sugar and continue to cook over low heat for about 10 more minutes, or until apples are soft.

Mascarpone Cheese
This is the sweet cream cheese popular throughout Italy. It can be obtained at most Italian delis or cheese counters. Whip in a little cinnamon and brown sugar, or toasted chopped pistachios or pecans. This makes a perfect spread for scones, bagels, muffins, etc. (If mascarpone is impossible to find, substitute regular cream cheese, softened.)

A Trio of Souffles

Souffles are a perfect choice for an entertaining brunch and despite their reputation, they are not really that difficult to make. Here are some tips for success:

* Have egg whites at room temperature
* Use a very clean metal mixing bowl. Make sure there are no specks of oil of any kind on the surface. (Avoid plastic bowls—they attract grease.)
* Beat the whites slowly at first, creating lots of bubbles
* Use a good strong electric beater or a balloon type wire whisk.
* Once the egg whites start to hold their peaks and are smooth and creamy you are ready to fold in the rest of the ingredients. The whites should be stiff but still moist. Do not overbeat.
* The souffle dish should be well greased and dusted with bread crumbs, cheese or sugar (for a dessert souffle). The coating allows the mixture to cling to the dish and rise high. After coating the dish, chill it in the refrigerator. A cold dish will help the souffle rise evenly.
* Prepare all the sauces etc. and have ready at room temperature before you beat the whites. Then fold the whites gently into the sauce mixture, adding a little at a time. Pour into the cold souffle dish and pop into the oven. Don't open the oven door to check on its progress or it will fall. When cooked, the souffle should be golden and firm to the touch.
* A good souffle is worth waiting for. Make sure the guests are ready to eat as soon you bring the souffle to the table.
* Preheat the oven to 400 degrees F. (200 degrees C.), then reduce to 375 degrees F. (190 degrees C.) just before you put in the souffle.

Something To Celebrate, page 81. Clockwise from top: Rack of Lamb, Oriental Fried Vegetable Rice, Peanut Satay Sauce, N.Y. Duck Salad, Wontons, Creme Brulee, Gin-Gingered Prawns.

Pasta, Pasta, Pasta!, page 93. Clockwise from top: Watermelon with Purple Onions, Assorted Italian Pissaladieres.

Orient Expression, page 101. Clockwise from top: Chocolate Sushi, Shrimp Crackers, Chilled Champagne Melon Soup, Asian Salad with Grilled Chicken Strips.

Cross-Culture Cuisine, page 106. Clockwise from top: Spicy Noodles with Prawns & Pork, Asparagus with Peanut Dressing, Strawberry Rhubarb Torte.

Barb Vance's Mushroom Souffle

Barb's souffle was first served at a luncheon for our Gourmet 8 group in 1968, making this recipe nearly a quarter of a century old. It's still just as popular. It makes a perfect dinner, along with a simple green salad. Serves 4 to 6.

2 cups (500 mL) finely chopped fresh mushrooms
6 tablespoons (90 mL) butter
¼ cup (60 mL) all purpose flour
1 cup (250 mL) warm milk
3 tablespoons (45 mL) chopped green onions
Pinch salt
Pepper to taste
¼ teaspoon (1 mL) dried thyme or dill
4 egg yolks
5 egg whites

On the day ahead, or early on the morning of serving, first prepare a 1½ quart (1.5 L) souffle dish by buttering well and dusting with fine breadcrumbs or grated Parmesan cheese. In a skillet, melt 2 tablespoons (30 mL) of the butter and saute the mushrooms for a minute or two. Set aside.

In a medium saucepan, melt the remaining butter, add flour and blend well. Remove from heat and add the warm milk a little at a time, stirring with wire whisk until smooth. Return to low heat and continue stirring for a few minutes until sauce is thickened. Add sauteed mushrooms, onions, salt, pepper and herbs, cover and leave to cool. Refrigerate.

Before baking, take out the mushroom mixture and bring to room temperature. Beat egg yolks until light and lemon coloured and fold into the mushroom mixture. Set aside. Preheat oven to 400 degrees F. (200 degrees C.)

Beat egg whites until they stand in stiff moist peaks, then carefully fold them, a little at a time, into the mushroom mixture. Turn into the chilled souffle dish and place dish in a pan of hot water: the water should come about 1½ inches (4 cms) up the sides of the dish.

Turn down oven to 375 degrees F. (190 degrees C.) and carefully slide in the souffle and water pan. Bake for about 45 minutes or until the souffle is golden and the centre is firm. Serve at once with the Cheddar Cheese sauce and steamed asparagus.

Cheddar Cheese Sauce

This sauce can be prepared the day ahead and reheated. If it's too thick, thin out with a little milk. It also freezes well. Vary the cheese for a change of flavour: try Swiss Emmentaler or Gruyere.

3 tablespoons (45 mL) butter
3 tablespoons (45 mL) flour
1½ cups (375 mL) warm milk
¾ cup (180 mL) grated sharp Cheddar cheese
½ teaspoon (2 mL) Dijon mustard
Pinch cayenne pepper
Pinch salt
Pepper to taste

Melt butter in a small saucepan. Add flour and blend well. Remove from stove and add the warm milk slowly, whisking with a wire whisk to keep smooth. Cook for a few minutes over low heat, stirring constantly, until thickened. Add remaining ingredients and blend well until cheese is melted. Cover, cool and refrigerate or freeze for future use.

Makes about 1½ cups (375 mL).

Crab Souffle

Elegant and airy, this crab souffle adds a sophisticated note for brunch or light dinner. It's best with fresh cooked crab, of course. (The cheese sauce also goes well with this.) Serves 4.

    3 tablespoons (45 mL) butter
    3 tablespoons (45 mL) flour
    1 cup (250 mL) warm milk
    3 tablespoons (45 mL) chopped green onion
    Salt and pepper to taste
    ¼ teaspoon (1 mL) Dijon mustard
    ½ cup (125 mL) Emmentaler or Gruyere cheese, grated
    1 cup (250 mL) fresh crabmeat, rinsed and picked over for shell
    4 egg yolks
    5 egg whites
    2 tablespoons (30 mL) Parmesan cheese

Prepare 1½ quart (1.5 L) souffle dish by buttering and coating with Parmesan cheese, then chilling. Preheat oven to 400 degrees F. (200 degrees C.)

In a small saucepan, melt the butter, add flour, stir for a few minutes, then remove from heat and gradually whisk in the warm milk. Return to low heat and continue to stir until mixture is thickened and smooth. Add onions, salt, pepper, mustard and cheese and stir until cheese is melted. This sauce can be made the day ahead, if desired and kept in the refrigerator.

Just before baking, gently rewarm the sauce, beat the egg yolks and fold in. Set aside to cool. Fold in the crabmeat.

Beat egg whites until stiff but not dry and fold a little at a time into the crab mixture. Pour into cold prepared souffle dish and sprinkle top with Parmesan cheese. Put souffle dish into a larger pan and pour in 1 to 2 inches (2.5 to 5 cms) of hot water. Turn down oven to 375 degrees F. (190 degrees C.) and bake souffle for about 35 to 40 minutes until firm and golden. Serve immediately.

Cheese and Rice Souffle

Another classic, this souffle is given a meaty consistency by the addition of cooked white rice. It goes well with grilled seafood or chicken.

Serves 4 to 6.

2 tablespoons (30 mL) butter
3 tablespoons (45 mL) flour
¾ cup (180 mL) warm milk
½ lb (250 g) sharp Cheddar cheese, grated
Pinches of salt and pepper to taste
1 cup (250 mL) cooked long grain white rice
4 large egg yolks
5 large egg whites

Preheat oven to 400 degrees F. (200 degrees C.) and butter and coat a 1½ quart (1.5 L) souffle dish with breadcrumbs or grated cheese. Make the sauce by melting the butter, adding flour, blending well, then whisking in the warm milk. Cook, stirring constantly, until thickened. Add cheese, and stir until cheese is melted. Add salt and pepper. Fold in the rice. Cool and cover. This can be made the day ahead if you wish.

Just before serving, reheat the cheese sauce and blend in the beaten egg yolks. Cool, set aside. Beat egg whites until stiff but not dry, then fold into the cheese and rice sauce very gently, adding a little of the whites at a time.

Turn into the prepared souffle dish, and make an indentation with the back of a spoon all around the top, about 1 inch (2.5 cm) from the edge. Set dish in a larger pan filled with 1 to 2 inches (2.5 to 5 cms) of hot water, turn down oven temperature to 375 degrees F. (190 degrees C.) and place souffle in the centre of oven to bake for about 35 to 40 minutes. Remove from oven when golden and firm to touch and serve immediately.

Break an Egg!

Everyone can make scrambled eggs but an omelette is something else. It's a challenge, an intriguing creation. And it must be done well.

The pan should be of heavy porous metal, such as cast iron, preferably about 10 inches (25 cm) in diameter, though a non-stick fry pan also works well. Heat the pan to just the right temperature: if a small lump of cold butter placed into the pan sizzles briskly without browning, then the pan is ready.

Do not beat the eggs too long. In fact, don't use an egg beater at all. This takes all the life out of the eggs, leaving them thin and tough when cooked. Thirty seconds with a good strong fork is ample beating for 6 eggs.

Do not add pepper to the eggs before cooking. Pepper will discolour and toughen the eggs.

One tablespoon (15 mL) of butter in the pan is enough for a 3 to 6 egg omelette. Let the butter come to a froth, wait until the bubbles burst, then pour in the eggs.

Stir for just a second with the flat of a fork. Let the omelette cook, lifing the eggs here and there to let the liquid run underneath. If you are folding the omelette, bring the left half to the centre while the centre is still soft, but make the third fold as you slide it out onto the serving plate.

For a basic omelette for two people you will need 6 eggs, 2 tablespoons (30 mL) water, pepper, salt, and 2 tablespoons (30 mL) butter.

Spanish Omelette

This combination of potatoes and eggs makes a perfect main course. You can also add a medium zucchini, thinly sliced and a crushed clove of garlic. Serves four generously.

3 medium potatoes
3 tablespoons (45 mL) safflower oil
½ cup (125 mL) chopped onions
Salt to taste
6 eggs
1 tablespoon (15 mL) cold water
1 teaspoon (5 mL) butter
Freshly ground black pepper
2 to 3 tablespoons (30 to 45 mL) grated Parmesan cheese

Peel and slice the potatoes as thinly as possible. Heat oil in frypan, add potatoes, onions and garlic (if used) and fry over high heat until golden. Cover, reduce heat and cook until tender, about 8 to 10 minutes. Add salt to taste.

Beat eggs lightly with fork, add cold water and pour into the potato onion mixture. Cook according to basic directions but don't fold. Slide out onto platter, sprinkle with pepper and Parmesan cheese and serve. Omelette can be kept warm for a few minutes in the oven.

Basque Omelette

This tasty ham and vegetable filling can be made well ahead of time. Make a plain omelette in the usual way, spread the sauce in the middle, fold in half and turn out onto a hot serving platter.   Serves 4 to 6.

2 tablespoons (30 mL) safflower oil
1 small onion, chopped
1 red pimento, diced
1 garlic clove, minced
1 ham slice, cut into long strips
2 peeled tomatoes, diced
¼ teaspoon (1 mL) thyme or basil or 1 tablespoon of fresh herbs
½ green or red pepper, cut into strips

Heat oil in frypan and add onion, pepper, pimento and garlic. Stir over high heat for 2 minutes, then add ham and tomatoes. Simmer for 20 minutes or until sauce is thick. Add thyme or basil, salt and pepper to taste.

Other Omelette Suggestions

To the basic 6 egg omelette add sauteed mushrooms, regular or wild, and grated Asiago and Monterey Jack cheese. For Mexican Style, add drained, chopped mild chili peppers, sliced avocado and grated Monterey Jack cheese, topped with sour cream and Mexican salsa.

Omelette in a Bread Box

A great idea for a late morning picnic or breakfast buffet. This is great with homemade relish or ketchup, and hot apple cider makes a perfect drink.
                                                                    Serves 6.

> 1 large round French or sourdough loaf, about 10 to 12 inches (25 to 30 cms) in diameter
> 1 tablespoon (15 mL) oil and melted butter combined
> Ingredients for Spanish Omelette, using 9 eggs

Just before serving (or leaving for the picnic), heat oven to 350 degrees F. (180 degrees C.) Cut the bread in half horizontally and partly hollow out the centre of each half, leaving about 1 inch (2.5 cm) of soft bread and crust. Brush the insides with the oil and butter. Reassemble loaf and wrap in heavy foil. Place in oven to heat while making omelette.

When omelette is set, remove bread from oven, open and slide the omelette into the bottom half of the bread "box". Quickly replace the top half of the "bread box", cut into wedges and serve immediately. For picnic use, leave whole and wrap very well in foil. It will keep warm for several hours. Slice just before serving.

Breakfast Tacos

A quick Mexican style omelette for an early morning pick-me-up.

Serves 2 to 4.

4 flour tortillas
2 tablespoons (30 mL) corn oil
1 tablespoon (15 mL) butter
8 extra large eggs, lightly beaten
3 tablespoons (45 mL) water
1 ripe avocado, cubed
1 cup (250 mL) grated jalapeno/Monterey Jack cheese (or plain Monterey Jack)
Pepper to taste
Mexican salsa

Warm tortillas in foil in a 350 degree F. (180 degree C.) oven for 5 to 10 minutes or until heated through. Slightly beat eggs and water.

In a skillet heat the corn oil and butter and cook the eggs slightly; fold in the avocado, cheese and pepper and cook until eggs are set. Lay warm tortillas out on warm plate, put eggs in the middle of each and roll up like jelly rolls, tucking ends under. Serve immediately with salsa.

Be prepared to make more!

Rainbow Inn Apple/Cream Cheese Crepes

Herb and Marianne Horen have a most delightful bed and breakfast inn at La Conner, Washington. During the spring flower season you wake up to fields of yellow daffodils and scarlet tulips outside the window. Breakfast on the verandah listening to the birds singing and talking to the other guests is a delight, particularly these luscious crepes. Serves 6.

Crepes
1½ cups (375 mL) water
½ cups (375 mL) cold milk
6 eggs
½ teaspoon (2 mL) salt
1¾ cups (430 mL) flour
6 tablespoons 90 mL) butter

Put liquids, eggs and salt into blender or mixer and blend until smooth. Add flour and butter and continue to blend until smooth. (Or use a large bowl and a wire whisk.) Cover batter and refrigerate for 2 hours. This step is important!

The batter should have the consistency of light cream, just thick enough to coat a wooden spoon. Heat small crepe skillet rubbed lightly with oil, and when it is smoking hot pour in about ¼ cup (60 mL) of the batter, tilting the pan in all directions so that the batter covers the bottom. Heat for about a minute, until the surface is almost dry, then quickly toss or flip over. Heat the flip side for about 30 seconds, then turn out onto a platter. Repeat until all batter is used up. This should make about 24 crepes. If it is more than you need, the cooked crepes freeze very well. A stack of crepes in the freezer could be the beginning of a great impromptu lunch.

Cream Cheese Filling
1 lb (450 g) cream cheese, softened
2 eggs
½ cup (125 mL) sugar
1 tablespoon (15 mL) fresh lemon juice
1 teaspoon (5 mL) vanilla
½ cup (125 mL) ground walnuts

Topping
⅓ cup (80 mL) butter
⅓ cup (80 mL) sugar
½ teaspoon (2 mL) cinnamon
Juice of ½ lemon
4 Granny Smith apples, peeled and very thinly sliced

Mix all the ingredients for the cream cheese filling, divide between 18 crepes, roll crepes up around filling. Melt half of the topping butter in a large shallow baking dish and sprinkle with half of the sugar. Place crepes, seam sides down, on top and dot with the remaining butter. Cover with apple slices, the rest of the sugar, cinnamon and lemon juice and bake for 15 minutes at 400 degrees F. (200 degrees C.) or until caramelized.

Family Favourites

"Component Cooking" may very well be the style for the 90s. This means a combination of home cooking and buying dishes from specialty food shops or delis. I rely on several specialty shops, including The Stock Market on Granville Island for stocks, pasta sauces, dressings and condiments; the Que Pasa Mexican market and several Gourmet Take Out establishments. They are my life savers. My motto is, if you can buy it as good or better than you could make it yourself, then go for it!

We all have our stock of treasured family recipes and old reliables that we depend on. Here are some from my files to add to yours:

Marinated Onions

This recipe has been in my file forever and is always popular for holiday entertaining. Roast a baron of beef to medium or medium rare, provide a dish of the onions and a basket of fresh buns and let guests help themselves. Note: a 6 lb (3 kilo) roast should serve 20 to 24. Slice thinly or shave the beef.

> 750 mL malt or cider vinegar
> 1 cup (250 mL) sugar
> 4 to 5 purple or white sweet onions, very thinly sliced
> 1 cup (250 mL) sour cream
> 1 cup (250 mL) mayonnaise
> 2 tablespoons (30 mL) celery seed

A day ahead of serving combine vinegar and sugar and stir until sugar has dissolved. Pour over onion slices and marinate overnight. The following day, drain onions well and squeeze until they are no longer watery. Blend sour cream, mayonnaise and celery seed in a bowl and fold in the onions. Refrigerate until you are ready to serve.

Cranberry and Pear Chutney

Barb Watts shares the same passion for food as I do. She has organized many of my cooking classes over the years and is always there when you need her. Her chutney recipe is our family's favourite. It's perfect for Christmas turkey, goose or duck and will keep for a week or so in the refrigerator. It can also be frozen.

2 cups (500 mL) cranberries
1 cup (250 mL) peeled and chopped pears
¼ cup (60 mL) raisins
2 tablespoons (30 mL) mulled wine spice
   (You can sometimes buy packets in kitchen shops)
1 cinnamon stick, broken
¾ cup (180 mL) white sugar
¼ cup (60 mL) port
¼ cup (60 mL) water
1 tablespoon (15 mL) fresh lemon juice.

Combine cranberries, pears and raisins in a large saucepan along with the sugar, lemon juice, port and water. Place spices in a cheese cloth bag and add. Bring mixture to a boil and simmer until sauce is thickened and fruit tender, about 15 to 20 minutes. Chill overnight. Remove spice bag.

Layered Vegetable Salad

Lily Richardson is noted for her grand dinner parties but she also enjoys hosting casual poolside buffets. This salad is one of her classics for barbecues or picnics.   Serves 8 to 10.

2½ cups (625 mL) frozen baby peas
1 head romaine lettuce, cut julienne
1 large or 2 small red peppers, seeded and chopped
1 medium white sweet onion, chopped finely
2 cups (500 mL) mayonnaise
1 teaspoon (5 mL) white sugar
1 cup (250 mL) grated Cheddar or Swiss cheese

Early on day of serving, blanch peas in boiling water for one or two minutes. Drain and cool by running under cold water; drain again and dry.

Line the bottom of a glass salad bowl with the shredded lettuce, then layer with the white onion, red pepper and peas. Spread mayonnaise over the top and sprinkle with the sugar. Top with grated cheese. Cover bowl with plastic wrap and refrigerate for at least 6 hours.

Mango-Tomato-Basil Salad

An unusual trio of tastes and colours that works. It makes an outstanding addition to a summer buffet. Make sure the tomatoes are at their sweetest and the mangoes really ripe.   Serves 4 to 6.

6 large ripe tomatoes
2 large ripe mangoes
1 bunch fresh basil, about ¾ cup (180 mL)

Slice tomatoes ½ inch (12mm) thick and cut the peeled mangoes into thin wedges. Just before serving, arrange tomatoes in overlapping circles to cover a large round platter. Intersperse with the wedges of mango and sprinkle liberally with fresh basil leaves. Add a dash of salt and drizzle over a little olive oil.

Salad Croutons

Commercial croutons cannot compare with the crispness and flavour of the ones you make yourself. They are easy to do, and it's an excellent way to use up leftover breads, rolls, bagels, etc. I save my leftovers, putting them in the freezer until I have enough bread for a batch of mixed croutons, and the time to make them. They're wonderful munchies.

> 4 to 6 cups (1 to 1.5 L) small bread cubes
> 4 to 5 large garlic cloves, peeled and chopped finely
> 1 cup (250 ml) Parmesan cheese
> About ½ cup (125 ml) olive oil

Toss bread cubes with the chopped garlic and spread out on a large ungreased cookie sheet. Sprinkle with Parmesan cheese and drizzle oil over the top, using enough to coat the bread cubes well. Bake at 250 degrees F. (120 degrees C.) for about 1 to ½ hours, stirring the cubes around from time to time. They should be golden.

You can test whether they are cooked through by dropping one into a cup of water: if it floats it's done, but if it sinks to the bottom then it needs more time in the oven. Cool on rack, then store in covered container in the refrigerator. They will keep fresh for weeks.

Potato Gratin Italian Style

A side dish to complement any meat or fish entree, this is one of the my classics. It can be served year-round and never fails to please.

Serves 6.

6 large potatoes, peeled and very thinly sliced
2 medium zucchini, thinly sliced
5 Roma tomatoes, sliced thinly (or 1 cup (250 mL) cherry tomatoes, halved)
6 tablespoons (60 mL) freshly grated Parmesan cheese
Oregano, basil, to taste
⅓ cup (80 mL) chicken stock
Olive oil

Line a large, well oiled, shallow casserole or gratin dish with a layer of sliced potatoes. Place a mixture of zucchini and tomato slices on top, sprinkle with cheese and herbs and drizzle over a little oil. Repeat the layers, ending with the cheese and herbs, and pour the chicken stock over the top.

Bake at 400 degrees F. (200 degrees C.) for about 40 minutes or until potatoes are tender. Serve immediately.

This dish can be cooked in advance and reheated for 30 minutes at 350 degrees F. (180 degrees C.) If you peel and slice the potatoes ahead of assembly, then keep them in ice water so they don't discolour, then drain and pat dry. The tomatoes and zucchini can also be peeled and sliced ahead of time.

Chicken Tortilla Pie

It's a standing joke in my family that almost every time Simon Hoogerwerf, Canada's premier 800 metre champion, drops over for dinner, I'm serving Mexican food! The athletes we know seem to crave Mexican food, perhaps because it is high in carbohydrates and it is filling and fortunately Simon is no exception. I call this dish my Mexican Lasagne. It can be made a day ahead if you wish and reheated before serving. To complete the hearty menu, add some deli food such as corn chips, salsa, guacamole and refried beans. The pie is quick to make and freezes well. It's great for ski weekends. Serves 8.

2 tablespoons (30 mL) vegetable oil
½ cup (125 mL) onions, finely chopped
2 garlic cloves, finely chopped
2 (125 mL) cans mild green chilies, drained and chopped
1 cup (250 mL) enchilada or picante sauce
1 (7½ oz, 213 mL) can tomato sauce
1 cup (250 mL) chicken broth
1 cup (250 mL) milk
2 cups (500 mL) Monterey Jack cheese, grated
3 cups (750 mL) cooked chicken or turkey, in strips
18 corn tortillas
1 cup (250 mL) grated old Cheddar cheese

Heat oil in frypan and saute onions and garlic for a few minutes. Add chilies, sauces, broth, milk and jack cheese and stir until cheese is melted. Add chicken or turkey strips.

Place six tortillas in the bottom of a greased 13 by 19-inch (33 by 23 cm) pan. Cover with a third of the chicken mixture and cover with another layer of tortillas. Repeat, ending with a layer of sauce on top. Sprinkle with Cheddar cheese. Bake at 325 degrees F. (160 degrees C.) for about 30 to 40 minutes. Cool and refrigerate. Reheat at 350 degrees F. (180 degrees C.), covered with foil, for about 30 minutes or until hot. Remove foil for the last few minutes of cooking.

Mexicali Chicken

Another quick recipe to dress up with deli extras for rave reviews.

Serves 6 to 8.

> 8 single chicken breasts, boned and skinned
> 2 avocados
> 1 teaspoon (5 mL) lemon juice
> Chili powder to taste
> Pepper to taste
> 3 medium tomatoes, thinly sliced
> About a dozen thin slices of Monterey Jack cheese (enough to cover chicken)
> 3 to 4 tablespoons (45 to 60 mL) canned mild chili peppers, chopped
> Thin slices of red, green or yellow peppers (enough to cover chicken)

Saute chicken in butter about three minutes on each side. Cool. Peel and pit the avocados and mash well with lemon juice, chili powder and pepper. Place chicken breasts in a single layer on a cookie sheet. Cover with thin layers of first the mashed avocado, then the tomato slices, cheese slices, chili peppers and red and green peppers. Slip pan under the broiler and cook until the cheese melts.

Poulet Basquaise

On our recent trip to Turkey we met a delightful couple from the Basque region of France. Jacques and Maile Lenoir sent along the recipe for a traditional dish that they serve often. New green beans and baby potatoes or rice would be good accompaniments. The dish can be made a day ahead and freezes well. You will notice that no herbs are used. Instead the peppers and tomatoes are spiked with lots of garlic and pepper. Serves 6.

4 lb (2 kilo) roasting chicken.

Sauce
2 tablespoons (30 mL) olive oil
4 red, yellow or orange peppers, cut in julienne strips
2 medium onions, sliced
6 large cloves of garlic, chopped finely
2 lbs (1 kilo) tomatoes, peeled, seeded and coarsely chopped
Pinch of salt
Freshly ground pepper
½ cup (125 mL) dry white wine

Rub chicken with a little olive oil, sprinkle with salt and pepper and roast at 350 degrees F. (180 degrees C.) for about 90 minutes or until tender. Remove skin and cut cooked chicken into large serving pieces.

While the chicken is cooking, heat the olive oil in a heavy skillet and add peppers, onions and garlic. Saute for a few minutes, then add tomatoes, salt, pepper and wine. Simmer for 20 to 25 minutes or until the sauce thickens. Add the chicken pieces and simmer for a few more minutes. Serve hot immediately, or cool, refrigerate and reheat at 350 degrees F. (180 degrees C.) just until heated through.

Art Phillips'
Championship Meatloaf

Art Phillips and Dave Abbott both claimed they made the world's best meatloaf. So Carole Taylor, Art's wife, decided to put them to the test. She invited them to hold a bake-off and asked a few friends around to be judges. Included in the contest was actor Jackson Davies, the Beachcombers policeman, whose reputation as a cook was, to say the best, dubious.

Dave and Jackson arrived with their entries while Art slaved away in the kitchen putting the finishing touches to his masterpiece. Jackson's entry was disqualified at once: his loaf pan contained two Big Macs, but the final outcome between the two serious contenders was hard to decide. Then Art's artful work in the kitchen paid dividends. He emerged as the triumphant gold medalist. This is his recipe. It makes two loaves, each serving 6.

2 eggs
3 cups (750 mL) whole wheat breadcrumbs
1 large onion, minced
1 green pepper, minced
6 tablespoons (90 mL) horseradish
1 375 mL jar spaghetti sauce
1 tablespoon (15 mL) dry mustard
3 lbs (1.5 kilo) extra-lean ground beef

Beat eggs lightly in large bowl. Add all the other ingredients and mix well; finally stir in the ground beef. Divide into two and pack into oiled meatloaf pans and place in a preheated 400 degree F. oven (200 degrees C.) Remove one pan after 30 minutes, allow to cool, cover with aluminum foil and freeze for future use. Remove second pan after 45 minutes and serve.

Garlic Mashed Potatoes

Nothing goes better with meatloaf than mashed potatoes. I've updated them somewhat by adding loads of garlic. Add steamed carrots and peas and you have a classic family supper.   Serves 6.

8 large potatoes, peeled and quartered
4 to 5 large cloves of garlic, peeled
Salt to taste
Boiling water
2 tablespoons (30 mL) butter, optional
Milk or cream
Pepper

Put potatoes, garlic and salt into a large pot and cover with boiling water. Simmer until potatoes and garlic are both tender, drain well and mash. Add butter and milk and fluff up to the desired consistency. Add pepper to taste.

Pork Tenderloin Superb

A last minute life-saver, this pork dish goes back to my first cooking class over 20 years ago. I dedicate it to all my students, particularly those who have continued to ask for it over the years.   Serves 6 to 8.

    3 to 4 pork tenderloins (each about 1½ lbs, 2½ kilos)
    ½ cup (125 mL) soy sauce
    ½ cup (125 mL) rye whisky or Bourbon
    4 tablespoons (60 mL) brown sugar
    Dijon mustard
    Toasted sesame seeds

Trim and clean tenderloins and marinate in a mixture of the soy sauce, whisky and sugar for 2 to 3 hours. Drain, (reserve marinade), rub with a little Dijon mustard and roll in toasted sesame seeds to coat well. Bake at 375 degrees F. (190 degrees C.) for 25 to 30 minutes or until tender, basting with the reserved marinade from time to time.

To serve, slice thinly on the diagonal and serve with Mustard Sauce. Oriental Fried Vegetable Rice would make a good accompaniment. (See page 89.)

Mustard Sauce
    1 cup (250 mL sour cream
    1 cup (250 mL) mayonnaise
    1 tablespoon (15 mL) Dijon mustard
    4 tablespoons (60 mL) chopped green onion
    Juice of ½ lemon
    Pepper to taste

Blend well together. This can be made a day ahead.

Pavlova

Named for the famous ballerina, Pavlova is New Zealand's own famous dessert. It's so simple: merely a luscious marshmallow meringue topped with whipped cream and fresh fruit, but it's so delicious. When Doug and I were in New Zealand recently we enjoyed it often. Serves 6.

6 large egg whites
¼ teaspoon (1 mL) cream of tartar
Pinch of salt
1¼ cups (300 mL) berry sugar
1 tablespoon (15 mL) cornstarch
1 tablespoon (15 mL) white vinegar
1 teaspoon (5 mL) vanilla

Beat egg whites, cream of tartar and salt until stiff. Add sugar, a spoonful at a time, and continue to beat until the sugar is dissolved before adding more. Continue to beat until meringue is really thick and glossy. Fold in the cornstarch, vinegar and vanilla. On a cookie sheet lined with aluminum foil or cooking parchment spread out the meringue into a 7-inch (18 cm) circle. It will be about 2 inches (5 cms) high. Bake in a preheated 250 degree F. oven (120 degree C.) for 40 to 50 minutes, then turn oven temperature down to 200 degrees F. (100 degrees C.) and continue to bake for a further 10 minutes. The Pavlova should be crispy on the outside and a pale gold in colour. Cool, turn out onto a large plate and refrigerate. It may crack a little but it will be covered with the whipped cream. This can be made a day ahead.

Topping
2 cups (500 ml) whipping cream
1 teaspoon (5 mL) icing sugar
1 teaspoon (5 mL) vanilla
Beat together until thick.

To assemble pavlova, spread whipped cream topping on top and sides of meringue and decorate with lots of sliced fresh strawberries, mango and kiwi fruit, or the fruit of your choice.

Strawberries with Black Pepper

An unusual combination that is shockingly delicious. Don't be afraid to try it out on your guests. Serves 6.

Vanilla ice cream
2 cups (500 mL) strawberries, sliced thickly
2 tablespoons (30 mL) butter
⅓ cup (80 mL) orange juice
⅓ cup (80 mL) white sugar
3 tablespoons (45 mL) Pernod or Sambuca liqueur
1 teaspoon (5 mL) freshly ground black pepper, or to taste

Heat butter in a medium-sized skillet or chafing dish. Add orange juice and sugar and simmer for a few minutes to glaze and caramelize slightly. Add sliced strawberries and stir over medium heat until they are slightly softened. Sprinkle with the pepper, pour over the liqueur and set it alight, shaking the pan until the flames die out. Serve the strawberries over scoops of vanilla ice cream.

Oriental Express Ice Cream

Serve in a cookie basket or in a wine goblet for a quick exotic dessert.
Serves 6 to 8.

6 to 8 scoops of coffee ice cream
2 to 3 fresh mangoes, peeled and sliced or 1 can (14 oz, 398 mL) mangoes, sliced
1 can (19 oz, 540 mL) Chinese lychee nuts, drained
4 tablespoons (60 mL) toasted slivered almonds or chopped macadamia nuts
10 tablespoons (150 mL) coffee liqueur

Marinate half the mangoes in 7 tablespoons (105 mL) of the liqueur for 2 to 3 hours in the refrigerator. Puree the rest of the mangoes with the rest of the liqueur. Chill.

To serve: Place a scoop of ice cream in goblet or cookie basket and surround it with 3 pieces of mango and 3 lychee nuts. Pour over a little mango puree and top with a sprinkle of nuts.

Red Velvet Cake

This recipe really is an oldie! It first appeared in our family as the Coronation Cake because it was served as a birthday cake at around the time when Queen Elizabeth was crowned. Its vibrant red colour makes it unique. Don't be alarmed by the amount of food colouring (unless you're allergic to it); the texture is smooth and moist. It's a cake for a very special occasion. Try it for Valentine's Day.

½ cup (125 mL) shortening
1½ cups (375 mL) white sugar
2 eggs
2 teaspoons (10 mL) cocoa
¼ cup (60 mL) red food colouring
½ teaspoon (2 mL) salt
1 teaspoon (5 mL) vanilla
1 cup (250 mL) buttermilk
1½ teaspoons (7 mL) white vinegar
1 teaspoon (5 mL) baking soda
2½ cups (725 mL) cake flour

Cream shortening, sugar and eggs. Make a paste with the cocoa and food colouring and add to the mixture. Blend salt and vanilla with buttermilk, add vinegar and baking soda, then add this to the egg mixture alternately with the flour. Pour into two 8-inch (20 cms) round cake pans which have been well greased and floured and bake at 350 degrees F. (180 degrees C.) for about 30 minutes or until the cake tests done. Cool. Sandwich together with some of the icing, then frost the top and sides.

Icing
5 tablespoons (75 mL) flour
1 cup (250 mL) milk
1 cup (250 mL) white sugar
1 cup (250 mL) butter
1 teaspoon (5 mL) vanilla

In a small saucepan blend flour and milk and cook until thickened, about 6 minutes, stirring constantly. Chill until cold. In a separate bowl cream the butter, sugar and vanilla, then fold in the cold flour custard. Cream together well. It may look curdled at first but soon it will take on the texture of whipped cream.

Chocolate Pear Bread Pudding

Don't turn your nose up at bread pudding. There is nothing so comforting during the cold winter months and this particular marriage of chocolate and pears elevates the humble dessert to gourmet heights. I predict we will be seeing more bread puddings in the 90s as the focus turns towards down-home cooking. This pudding is made in a loaf pan which gives it something of the look of a rich pate. Serve warm with a dollop of Creme Anglaise.   Serves 8 to 10.

4 eggs, slightly beaten
1 cup (250 mL) light cream
1 cup (250 mL) whole milk
½ cup (125 mL) white sugar
1 teaspoon (5 mL) vanilla
1 cup (250 mL) cocoa powder
1 loaf French bread, crusts removed, cubed (6 cups, 1.5 L)
½ cup (125 mL) unsalted butter
4 ripe pears, peeled, cored, chopped
4 tablespoons (60 mL) white sugar
Strawberries (optional)

In a large bowl, beat together the first six ingredients until smooth. Add the cubed bread and let it sit for about 30 minutes. Meanwhile, in a skillet, melt the butter, add the pears and the sugar and simmer together for 8 to 10 minutes until the pears are soft and tender.

Add the pears to the bread mixture, stirring well. Pour into a buttered loaf pan, then place into a larger shallow pan to which you have added about 2 inches (5 cms) of boiling water. Bake for about 50 to 60 minutes at 350 degrees F. (180 degrees C.) or until a knife inserted in the centre comes out clean and the top is firm. Let it sit a few minutes before turning pudding out onto a platter. Serve warm in ¼ inch (8 mm) thick slices, add some Creme Anglaise or vanilla yogurt and decorate with strawberries.

The pudding can be made the day ahead and reheated, covered, at 350 degrees F. (180 degrees C.) for about 15 to 20 minutes or until warm.

Christmas Pudding

Geoff and Rhoda Gowan invited me to their Ottawa home for an evening of tradional English cuisine, roast beef and Yorkshire pudding in all their splendour. The crowning glory was Rhoda's family plum pudding. It was absolutely scrumptious. I acquired the recipe (of course) and now it's standard fare every Christmas in our house, too.

Geoff is a CBC TV sports commentator for athletics and every time I watch his broadcast I'm reminded of that wonderful plum pudding.

This recipe makes one large pudding. I recommend that you double the ingredients and make two, one for Christmas and one to freeze for later on. It's a shame to limit this wonderful taste to once a year.

Plum Pudding is traditionally served with Rum Hard Sauce (see Chef on the Run, page 150) but really a simple Creme Anglaise is all it needs.

The list of ingredients is intimidating, but really it's easy to make. One pudding serves 12 well. It is rich and filling.

5 heaping tablespoons (75 mL) all purpose flour
1 teaspoon (5 mL) baking powder
¼ teaspoon (2 mL) salt
10 heaping tablespoons (150 mL) fresh breadcrumbs
1 teaspoon (5 mL) cinnamon
½ teaspoon each (2 mL) nutmeg and ginger
6 oz (170 g) shredded suet
½ lb (225 g) currants
½ lb (225 g) golden raisins
½ lb (225 g) chopped muscatel raisins
3 oz (85 g) chopped mixed peel
¼ lb (225g) Demerara sugar
2 oz (60 g) slivered almonds
4 tablespoons (60 mL) golden corn syrup
1 small carrot, grated
3 eggs
Grated rind and juice of 1 orange
Grated rind and juice of 1 lemon
2 tablespoons (30 mL) milk
4 tablespoons (60 mL) rum or brandy

Mix together all dry ingredients, including suet, in a very large bowl. Add dried fruit, grated carrot, and orange and lemon rind. In a separate bowl, beat together the eggs with the syrup, juice, milk and spirits and stir this into the large bowl of dry ingredients, making a wish as you stir. (In our house, all family members are asked to take a turn with the wooden spoon and make a wish.) If you want to be traditional, wash a silver coin (a dime, nickel or quarter) and wrap in waxed paper. Spoon pudding mixture into large basin, burying coin deep in the centre. (Whoever finds the coin in his pudding on Christmas day will have lots of luck.)

Cover bowl with lid of cheese cloth or waxed paper allowing room for expansion and lower pudding basin onto a steaming rack in a large pot. Pour boiling water into the pot until it reaches about a third of the way up the pudding basin. Simmer gently for 3 to 4 hours. Store in a cool place (or the freezer) for several months. It improves with age.

To serve, simmer gently for a further 3 hours and bring to the table flaming with warmed brandy.

Creme Anglaise

This classic dessert sauce is rich and should be served in small portions for a special treat. It will keep in the refrigerator for several days. Makes about 1¾ cups (430 mL).

4 egg yolks
⅓ cup (80 mL) white sugar
1½ cups (375 mL) whole milk
½ teaspoon (2 mL) vanilla

In a heavy saucepan combine yolks and sugar, beating until thick and lemon coloured. Add milk slowly, beating well. Put over low heat and stir constantly until custard is slightly thickened. It should coat a wooden spoon. Add vanilla.

Global Food

Italian olive oil, Russian caviar, Oriental mushrooms, exotic fruits from Thailand and Mexico, olives from Greece—the world is fast becoming our supermarket. Ethnic and specialty markets are a continual source of culinary inspiration as we tease our tastebuds. To bring you up to date on the latest food trends, here is a glossary explaining a few of the specialty ingredients the recipes in this book use.

Chinese Chili Sauce—used to give a spicy tang to Oriental dishes. It's made with chilies, rice vinegar, garlic and salt. I prefer the milder blend but some like it hot. Use whatever your taste buds decide.

Chili Peppers—indispensable for fiery Mexican and Oriental dishes. The intensity of chilies vary; generally, the smaller they are, the milder they will be. The seeds are the hottest parts. Split the chilies and remove the seeds, using rubber gloves. The two most common in the markets are the California Anaheim and the Poblano, both light green and ranging from hot to mild. The most commonly used hot chilies are the Serrano and the Jalapeno, which are dark green, small, thin and HOT. Fresh chilies do not store well. Buy them only when you plan to use them right away.

Pepper—I use a mixture of three to four different peppers for an interesting taste, including black, white, green and red. Grind them together and use instead of regular black pepper.

Szechuan Peppercorns—From the province of Szechuan in China, these are available at most specialty and Oriental markets. They are stronger and more aromatic than black peppercorns, but not so hot. Before you use them, heat in a small skillet without oil for a few minutes, just until they start to smoke. Cool, then grind finely and add to sauces, rice dishes, etc. They give a unique flavour.

Coconut Milk—Commonly used in Thai cuisine, this milk can be easily obtained in cans in most Oriental markets. The Thai brand contains unsweetened coconut, water and a preservative. Stir well before using in peanut sauces, or as part of the liquid in rice dishes. The coconut flavour is subtle.

Cilantro—also known as coriander or Chinese parsley, has a distinctive pungent flavour that most people either love or hate. Use it sparingly if you are uncertain of your guests' tastes. It is used fresh in dishes from around the world. Buy it at your herb counter—or grow your own.

To store fresh herbs, place sprigs in a glass of water, cover with a plastic bag and refrigerate. They will keep fresh for several days. Or chop the herbs, place about 1 tablespoon (15 mL) into an ice cube compartment, fill with water and freeze. Store frozen herb cubes in plastic bags. The herbs will turn black but the flavour will remain fresh for months. Pop the frozen cubes into soups, stocks or marinades.

Curry Powder—Widely available, the best are found in specialty or Indian food stores. Experiment to find a blend that you like. Start with a mild blend and work up towards a stronger. The Thai Blend and Sharwoods are excellent.

Ginger Root—Of all the Oriental flavours, fresh ginger has the most universal appeal. It adds zest and freshness to any dish with its sharp bite and aromatic flavour. Thai ginger is harder in texture, lighter in colour and has a more delicate taste. When buying ginger root, look for a smooth, shiny surface. If it's dark and wrinkled, then it's not fresh. It will keep well in the refrigerator or dark cupboard for a week; for longer storage, slice it and place it in a glass jar, cover it with sherry and refrigerate. Use sparingly. (Dried, powdered ginger will give you an entirely different flavour.)

Hoisin Sauce—Used to accent the flavours in stir-fry dishes, barbecue sauces, this basically consists of soya beans, flour, vinegar, chili and spices.

Krupuk—also popular in Indonesian cuisine, these crisp wafers puff up when deep fried. They are often made from shrimp and are widely available in Oriental stores.

Oyster Sauce—I often use this slightly salty thick brown sauce in vegetable stir fry dishes. It contains oyster juice, sugar, water and caramel. For a quick appetizer, quicklky saute strips of raw beef filet and peeled prawns for a few minutes until cooked. Add oyster sauce to coat well and serve on cocktail picks.

Rice—There are so many different kinds of rice to choose from these days. Look for Chinese long grain rice in specialty markets. I also enjoy Japanese short grain, which is stickier, and the fragrant Thai rice.

Sesame Oil—This is not an oil for frying but to add to a dish for its flavour. Look for pure Oriental sesame oil which is dark in colour.

Soy Sauce, Dark and Light—What is the difference? Dark soy sauce contains molasses and has a more intense flavour; it will give a darker colour to a dish. I prefer the thinner, light soy sauce—which does not mean that it has less salt. If you want less salt, look for low sodium soy sauce.

Parmesan Cheese—Once you get a taste of the real thing, freshly grated, you will never want to go back to using second best. Most cheese shops carry the world's best, known as Parmigiano Reggiano, the Rolls-Royce of Parmesans from north-central Italy. It's well worth the extra pennies for its taste is unsurpassed. This cheese is made under strict government control only in certain regions of Italy and only between April 1 and November 11 when milk is at its best. It's always made by hand. To check if you're getting the real thing, ask to see the words Parmigiano-Reggiano etched in dots in the rind.

Romano, Pecorino and Fontina—Three excellent Italian cheeses, sharp taste, suitable for grating. Try them as a change from Parmesan.

Asiago—Another Italian cheese with a nutty flavour, it's excellent for grating and adding to pasta, and makes a nice change from Parmesan.

Mozzarella—A semi-soft cheese with a mild flavour and a low melting point, ideal for pizza and lasagne.

Chevre or Goat Cheese—Lower in fat than most cheeses and with a sharp tang. The Canadian Snow Goat cheese is a good one to start with because it is not as strong as most of the French varieties.

Olive Oil—If you've been feeling guilty about using olive oil, don't! Many medical studies done on cooking fats have shown that olive oil, a monounsaturate, is effective in lowering blood cholesterol levels. It is also claimed that if you swallow a spoonful of the oil before an evening of celebrating, it will prevent a hangover. No guarantees, though. Always try to keep two grades of olive oil on hand: a more expensive extra virgin (made from the first pressing of the olives) for salads and a more reasonable pure olive oil for cooking. Greek virgin olive oils, which are also very good, tend to be a bit cheaper.

Balsamic Vinegar—My all-time favourite vinegar, this is made from the juice of grapes aged at least 10 years in Italy, and blended in wooden casks with other vinegars that have been aged up to 50 years. All balsamic vinegar is a blend of younger and older vintages. The very best is produced in the province of Reggiano and labelled "Traditional Reggiano", but there are less expensive substitutes.

To make a Balsamic Vinaigrette Dressing, whisk together ½ cup (125 mL) olive oil with 2 to 3 tablespoons (30 to 45 mL) balsamic vinegar, ½ teaspoon (2 mL) Dijon mustard and pepper to taste. For variation, add 3 to 4 tablespoons (45 to 60 mL) chopped green onions or shallots, 2 tablespoons (30 mL) grated Parmesan cheese and 1 teaspoon (15 mL) of fresh herbs, such as oregano, basil or thyme.

Garlic—Abandon the powders, salts and pastes and go for the fresh. Choose garlic bulbs that are pinkish in colour and firm to the touch. Elephant garlic, the jumbo-size white bulbs now available in our markets is sweeter and less pungent and is becoming popular. Try it roasted and squeezed onto slices of French bread.

Pasta Power—Pasta has come a long way! You name it, any flavour you want from pumpkin to squid ink and every shape and size from rice-look-alike orzo to giant tubes and seashells. It's here to stay. The average North American eats about 40 pounds of pasta a year, catching up to the Italian average of 100 pounds. Which is best, fresh or dried? For cream sauces I prefer to use fresh, but good quality Italian dried pasta is better for tomato-based sauces. Be sure the dried brand you use is made from 100% semolina or durum wheat, which is the best quality flour for texture and flavour. For hearty tomato sauces, try the tubular pastas such as penne, rigatoni or ziti for a change.

How to Cook Pasta—Use a large deep pot that can hold about 6 quarts (6 L) of water for each pound of pasta. The more water you use, the less gummy the cooked pasta will be. Bring the water to a hard rolling boil, add 1 to 2 tablespoons (15 to 30 mL) oil, then add the pasta in small batches, stirring after each addition with a large wooden fork, gently separating the strands. When all pasta is added, make sure it is submerged in the water to cook evenly. Some Italian chefs say: "Never put oil in the pasta water". Take your choice.

Fresh pasta cooks very fast—allow between 2 to 5 minutes. Dried pasta will take longer, from 8 to 15 minutes. To tell whether it is cooked to your liking, keep tasting it. When ready the pasta should be still firm and chewy. Others may like it softer.

Drain immediately. Do not rinse unless the pasta is to be used in a cold salad or you are going to toss it in an oil marinade. Rinsing in cold water will remove the starches which make the sauce cling to the pasta.

Pasta Leftovers—Put a little olive oil in a skillet over medium heat and add the cooked leftover pasta. Beat 2 to 3 eggs and pour over the pasta and sprinkle with salt and pepper. When bottom is golden, turn pasta pancake over and cook on the other side. Sprinkle with Parmesan cheese to serve.

Dried pasta can be stored indefinitely without any loss in quality; cooked or fresh pasta must be frozen for later use. To cook, drop it into boiling water straight from the freezer.

Tomatoes—One of the great additions to the culinary world, the tomato originated in the New World where it was discovered by the Spanish and brought to Europe, at first purely as an ornamental plant. Imagine cooking today without tomatoes!

Fresh tomatoes are the diamonds in Italian cuisine, but when they are out of season, even the Italians will confess to using canned tomatoes. Lorenza de Medici, who heads one of the most prestigious cooking schools in Tuscany, passes this trick along. When the plum tomatoes are at their peak, pop them into a plastic freezer bag, squeeze out excess air and freeze them whole. When ready to use, dunk the tomatoes into a large bowl of cold water for 15 to 20 seconds. The skins will slip off easily and you're ready to make a fresh tomato sauce any time of the year.

Sun-Dried Tomatoes—Great to have on hand, these dried roma tomatoes, usually preserved in olive oil, have an intense flavour that will turn a simple pasta dish into a masterpiece. Soak whatever you need in boiling water for about 10 minutes, drain, drizzle with a little olive oil and chop. Most Italian delis sell them already marinated in oil. I buy these as I need them.

Toasted Nuts—I always try to keep one or two varieties such as pine nuts, almonds or pecans on hand to add to salads, entrees, desserts, etc. Toasting them brings out the flavour. Put the nuts on an ungreased cookie sheet and bake in the oven at 350 degrees F. (180 degrees C.) for 5 to 7 minutes until they are golden. Check them frequently.

A Well-stocked Pantry

The phone rings. "When did you arrive in town? Love to see you. Drop over for dinner tonight."

What will I serve, there's nothing in the fridge! Panic sets in.

Sounds familiar? There comes a time when a well-stocked pantry and freezer will save the day—and keep your blood pressure down. For last minute guests I keep on hand the makings for one easy dinner. I find that Italian, Chinese and Mexican ingredients have often come to my rescue for an impromptu meal. Here are my stock-up list suggestions:

The Cupboard
    Assorted pastas
    Sun-dried tomatoes
    Olive and safflower oils
    Vinegars, including red and white wine, balsamic and champagne
    Canned roasted red peppers
    Garlic
    Dried herbs and spices: basil, oregano, thyme, rosemary, cinnamon, whole nutmeg, paprika, coriander, tarragon, cumin, turmeric, chili powder, curry powder
    Dried crushed red pepper flakes
    Anchovies
    Canned chunk tuna
    Marinated artichoke hearts
    Olives: black, green, Greek
    Garbanzo beans
    Italian amaretti biscuits and ladyfingers
    Canned Italian white or pinto beans
    Canned tomatoes
    Tomato sauce
    Tomato paste
    Mustard: Dijon, country style
    Rice: Arborio, brown or basmati, long-grain white, Bulgur wheat for pilaf, wild and Thai rice
    Chicken broth
    nuts: pecans, almonds, hazelnuts, pine nuts
    Jams and jellies

Pure maple syrup
Dried mushrooms: shiitake, porcini
Water chestnuts
Krupuk & rice crackers
Hoisin sauce
Plum sauce
Light & dark soy sauce
Chili sauce
Coconut milk
chutneys
Canned mangoes
Sesame oil
Chinese crispy noodles
canned baby corn
canned bamboo shoots
canned green chilies
canned salsa
canned refried beans
tortilla chips
Piquant or enchilada sauce

The Freezer
Whenever I'm cooking for a dinner party, I try to make three times the quantities needed and freeze several extra dishes for future use. I also keep the freezer well supplied with my favourite deli or caterer's specials, including a dessert, a main course and an appetizer. In addition, I keep the following on hand:

Chicken breasts
Rock cornish game hens
Lamb chops
Pork tenderloin
Snow peas
Pizza crusts
Corn and flour tortillas
Pita bread
Wontons
Filo paper
Tiger prawns
Smoked salmon
Bread, baguette, multi-grain
Bagels
Pesto for pasta

Coffee beans
Brownies
Scones
Chocolate cake
Ice cream
Berries
Limeade, lemonade

Things to Freeze from the book
Appetizers: Spicy nuts
  Pecan cheese chips
  Italian Pissaladiere
Soup: Carrot Tomato
Entrees: Art Phillip's Meatloaf
  Chicken Tortilla Pie
  Chicken Artichoke Pie
  Moroccan Chicken
  Poulet Basquaise
  Lamb Shanks with Orzo
Condiments: Peanut Satay Sauce and dressing
  Tomato Sauce
  Mexican Pesto
Sweets: Brownie Torte
  Tarte au Citron
  Swiss Chocolate Fingers
  Almond Cookie Shells
  Cranberry and Banana Bread
  Coconut Meringue Cake
  Royal Chocolate Fingers
  Chocolate Ganache Torte
  Scones
  Morning Glory Muffins
  Red Velvet Cake
  Christmas Pudding
  Crepes

Index of Recipes

Angela Pia	100	Ruth Matheson's Morning	
Annette's Vinaigrette Dressing	23	Glory Muffins	115
APPETIZERS		Breakfast Tacos	133
Asparagus with Peanut		Bruschetta	4
Dressing	107	Buttermilk Pancakes, Gold Medal	118
Baked Brie	11		
Bruschetta	4	California Sandwich Bake	114
Crostini	4	Cantonese Dressing	65
Gin-Gingered Prawns	84	Carrot Salad	24
Italian Pissaladière	94	Carrot Tomato Soup	77
Pecan Cheese Crisps	45	Champagne Zabaglione	66
Pesto Crostini	5	Cheddar Cheese Sauce	126
Spicy Nuts	82	Cheese and Rice Souffle	128
Toasted Sesame/Chevre Crostini	6	Chicken and Artichokes in	
Triple Creme Cheese with		Filo Paper	78
Mangoes and Strawberries	11	Chicken, Grilled	61
Tzatziki	23	Chicken Tortilla Pie	141
Watermelon with Purple Onion	94	Chocolate Brownie Torte	34
Apple/Cream Cheese Crepes	134	Chocolate Fingers, Royal	19
Apricots and Dates, Stuffed	28	Chocolate Ganache Torte	48
Art Phillips' Championship		Chocolate Pear Bread Pudding	150
Meatloaf	144	Chocolate Sushi	104
Artichokes, how to cook and		Christmas Pudding	151
serve	59	Coconut Meringue Cake	57
Asian Salad	102	CONDIMENTS & SAUCES	
Asparagus with Peanut Dressing	107	Avocado Salsa	73
Avocado Oriental Salad	65	Cheddar Cheese Sauce	126
Avocado Salsa	73	Crab Cake Sauce	32
		Cranberry and Pear Chutney	137
Baked Brie	11	Creme Anglaise	152
Baked Peaches Stuffed with		Fruit Salsa	33
Amaretti Cookies	99	Lemon Butter Sauce	
Banana Bread, Margaret Rogers'	40	(for Asparagus)	47
Basque Omelette	131	Lemon Butter Sauce	
Beet Salad	24	(for Artichokes)	59
Bread Pudding, Chocolate Pear	150	Mango/Lime Sauce	60
BREADS, MUFFINS, ETC.		Mustard Dressing	33
Cranberry Loaf	116	Mustard Sauce	146
Focaccia Bread	68	Peanut Satay Sauce	91
Margaret Rogers' Banana Bread	40	Pommarola (Tomato Sauce)	98
Poppyseed Loaf	41	Quick Lomon Dill Mayonnaise	18
Raisin Scones	39	Red Pepper Chutney	61

Fresh Chef 161

Stock Market Chive Mayonnaise	18	Eggplant Salad	24
Stock Market Hot Mexican Pesto	74	Fitness Group Smoothie	37
Tomato and Pepper Relish	25	Focaccia Bread	68
Couscous with Chick Peas	27	French Toast, classic	112
Crab Souffle	127	French Toast, Dad's	113
Cranberry Loaf	116	Frittata Primavera	38
Creme Anglaise	152	Fruit Salsa	33
Creme Brulee, Vicki's	92		
Crostini de Mango and Prosciutto	6	Gin-Gingered Prawns	84
Crostini	4	Granola, Ruth's	117
Croutons for Salad	139	Grapes in White Chocolate	20
Cranberry and Pear Chutney	137	Greek Lemon Chicken	54
		Grilled Chicken Sandwich	32
Dad's French Toast	113	Grilled Chicken with Red Pepper Chutney	61
DESSERTS		Grilled Halibut	60
Almond Cookie Baskets	70	Grilled Vegetables	62
Angela Pia	100		
Apricots and Dates, Stuffed	28	Halibut, Grilled	60
Baked Peaches, Stuffed	99	Healthy Fruit Trifle	42
Champagne Zabaglione	66		
Chocolate Brownie Torte	34	Jack's Chocolate Brownie Torte	34
Chocolate Ganache Torte	48	Ju Ju Chocolate Sushi	104
Chocolate Pear Bread Pudding	150		
Chocolate Sushi	104	Lamb Shanks with Orzo	69
Christmas Pudding	151	Layered Vegetable Salad	138
Decadent Grapes in White Chocolate	20	Lemon Butter Sauce (for Asparagus)	47
Healthy Fruit Trifle	42	Lemon Butter Sauce (for Artichokes)	59
Ju Ju Chocolate Sushi	104	Lemon Chicken, Greek	54
Lime Angel Pie	80	Lemon Dill Mayonnaise	18
Mascarpone and Amaretto	28	Lemon Tart	63
Orient Expression Ice Cream	148	Lime Angel Pie	80
Pavlova	147	Lobster, Nova Scotia	17
Royal Chocolate Fingers	19		
Strawberries with Black Pepper	148	Mango Lime Sauce	60
Strawberry Rhubarb Tart	110	Mango-Tomato-Basil Salad	138
Tarte au Citron	63	Marinated Onions	136
Tiramisu	8	Mascarpone and Amaretto	28
Vicki's Creme Brulee	92	Mayonnaise	
Zabaglione	9	Stock Market Chive	18
Dianne's Rice Krispies Chocolate Chip Cookies	56	Quick Lemon Dill	18
		MEAT DISHES	
East Meets West Chicken	90	Lamb Shanks with Orzo	69

Meatloaf, Art Phillip's	144
Pork Tenderloin Superb	146
Meatloaf, Art Phillip's	144
Mexicali Chicken	142
Mexican Quesadillas	72
Morning Glory Muffins	115
Moroccan Roasted Chicken	26
Moroccan Vegetable Salad	55
Mushroom Souffle, Barb Vance's	125
Mustard Dressing	33
Mustard Sauce	146
New York Duck Salad	83
Noodles with Prawns and Pork	108
Nova Scotia Lobster	17
Omelette in a Bread Box	132
Onions, Marinated	136
Orient Expression Ice Cream	148
Oriental Fried Vegetable Rice	89
Oven French Fries	34
Pavlova	147
Peaches, Stuffed	99
Peanut Dressing	107
Peanut Satay Sauce	91
Pecan Cheese Crisps	45
Peppers with Fusilli	97
Pesto Crostini	5
Pesto Potato Salad	54
Pesto, Stock Market's Hot Mexican	74
Pissaladiere, Italian	94
Pommarolo (Tomato Sauce)	98
Poppyseed Loaf	41
Pork Tenderloin Superb	146
Potatoes, Garlic Mashed	145
Potato Gratin, Italian Style	140
POULTRY DISHES	
Chicken Tortilla Pie	141
Chicken Vegetable Saute	99
David's Chicken and Artichokes in Filo Paper	78
Duck Salad with Wontons	83
East Meets West Chicken	90
Greek Lemon Chicken	54

Grilled Chicken with Red Pepper Chutney	61
Grilled Chicken Sandwich	32
Moroccan Roasted Chicken	26
Poulet Basquaise	143
Roast Pheasant or Game Hens	46
Prawns, Grilled Tiger	66
Puttanesca	96
Poulet Basquaise	143
Quesadillas, Giant Mexican	72
Quick Crab Cake Sauce	32
Quick Lemon Dill Mayonnaise	18
Rack of Lamb (East Meets West)	90
Rainbow Inn	
Apple/Cream Cheese Crepes	134
Raisin Scones	39
Red Cabbage Salad with Feta	76
Red Pepper Chutney	61
Red Velvet Cake	149
Rice Krispies Chocolate Chip Cookies	56
Risotto al Frutti de Mare	7
Roast Pheasant	46
Ruth's Coconut Meringue Cake	57
Royal Chocolate Fingers	19
SALADS	
Asian	102
Avocado Oriental	65
Beet	24
Carrot	24
Eggplant	24
Layered Vegetable	138
Mango-Tomato-Basil	138
Moroccan Vegetable	55
New York Duck	83
Pesto Potato	54
Red Cabbage with Feta Cheese	76
Vegetable Julienne	30
Warm Spinach with Basil and Prosciutto	6
Warm Wild Mushroom	44
Wild Rice	12
Salad Croutons	139

Fresh Chef 163

SALAD DRESSINGS
   Annette's Vinaigrette   23
   Balsamic Vinaigrette   156
   Cantonese   65
   Ginger/Chutney   12
Sangria   72
SEAFOOD
   Crab Cakes   31
   Crab Souffle   127
   Gin-Gingered Prawns   84
   Grilled Tiger Prawns   66
   Nova Scotia Lobster   17
   Seafood Risotto   7
Spanish Omelette   130
Spicy Noodles with Prawns
   and Pork   108
Spicy Nuts   82
Spinach Salad with Basil
   and Prosciutto   6
Strawberries with Black Pepper   148
Strawberry Rhubard Tart   110
Stock Market Fresh Chive
   Mayonnaise   18
Stock Market Hot Mexican Pesto   74
Stuffed Peaches   99
Tacos, Breakfast   133
Tarte au Citron   63
Thai Rice with Coconut Milk   62
Toasted Sesame/Chevre Crostini   6
Tomato Pepper Relish   25
Tiramisu   8
Trifle, Healthy Fruit   42
Trimmings for Pancakes, etc.   119
Trio of Peppers Julienne   79
Triple Creme Cheese with
   Mangoes and Strawberries   11
Tzatziki   23

Valerio's Peppers with Fusilli   97
Vegetable Salad Julienne   30
Vegetables, Grilled   62

Warm Spinach Salad with
   Basil and Prosciutto   6
Warm Wild Mushroom Salad   44
Watermelon with Purple Onion   94
Wild Rice Salad   12
Wild Rice Stuffing   47

Yam Croutons   45

Zabaglione   9
Zabaglione, Champagne   66